The House of
Osama Bin Laden

Langlands & Bell

Thames & Hudson

6

709.22 LAN

The House of Osama Bin Laden

In October 2002 Ben Langlands & Nikki Bell spent two weeks in Afghanistan carrying out research for a commission awarded by the Imperial War Museum entitled *The Aftermath of September 11 and the War in Afghanistan*.

During their stay in the country Langlands & Bell visited a diverse range of locations including ISAF HQ (International Security Force for Afghanistan) the NATO derived task force led by the Turks at the time, the main American air base at Bagram, the site of the giant Buddhas at Bamyan, the Supreme Court in Kabul – to attend the first capital trial since the fall of the Taliban – and, after a long and difficult journey, the former home of Osama Bin Laden at Daruntah, where he lived for a period in the late 1990's.

After returning to London Langlands and Bell made a series of art works based on their experiences which they titled collectively *The House of Osama Bin Laden*. This book records Langlands & Bell's experiences in Afghanistan, together with the art works which resulted from their research commission *The Aftermath of September 11 and the War in Afghanistan*.

The House of Osama Bin Laden was first exhibited at the Imperial War Museum, London from 10 April – 26 May 2003 and at IMMA Irish Museum of Modern Art, Dublin from 10 December 2003 – 8 February 2004. Subsequently it has been shown in the exhibition *Friendly Fire* at TENT Rotterdam, and in the Turner Prize 2004 exhibition at Tate Britain. In February 2004 *The House of Osama Bin Laden* received the BAFTA award for Interactive Arts Installation for "the best installation by artists working with interactive digital media".

Afghan Diary

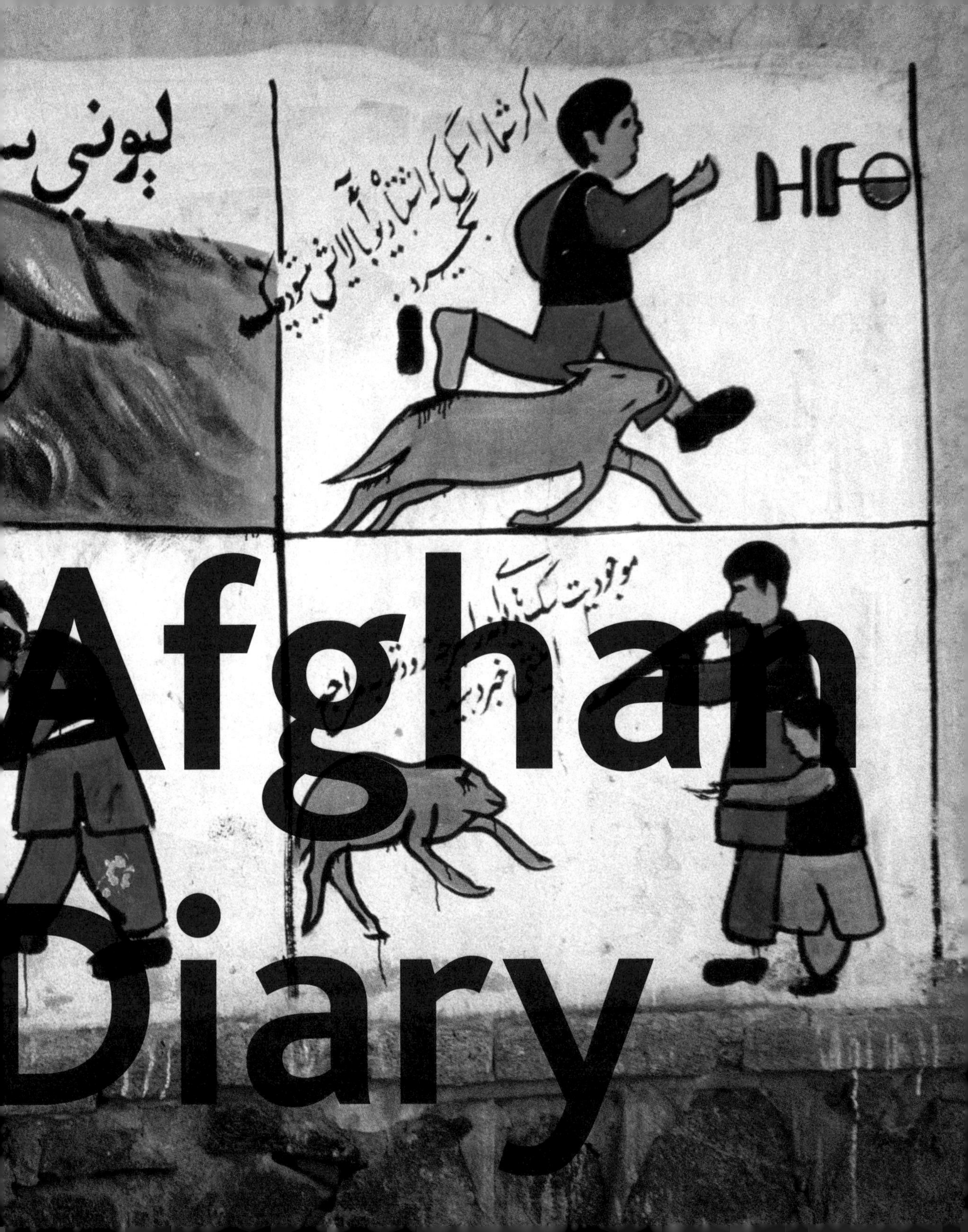

Friday 11 10 02

SHJ > KBL (Sharjah > Kabul)

We fly over some of the barest, driest, most mountainous, and apparently empty terrain we have ever seen. Suddenly Kabul appears in the distance like a scattering of debris swept to the edge of a plateau. We descend towards the airport where there is a heap of clutter beside the terminal building. It is a pile of Ariana (Afghan National Airlines) planes smashed by American bombing. Jim Williams of UNESCO has been waiting for us, returning to the airport for several days in a row. He takes us to the Mustafa Hotel. On the way he points out the US Embassy and the Presidential Palace over barricades of rubble filled

oil drums and sheets of impenetrable steel. Outside on the broken pavements of the avenues, Afghan sentries in shalwar kameez and woollen hats lie on broken charpoys with automatic rifles, grilling kebabs and brewing tea. When we arrive at the hotel we are told that the owner is in hospital having his stomach pumped because someone has tried to poison him. Jim tells us he has to leave Kabul for a few days on a mission and vanishes.

The Mustafa hotel is a three-storey reinforced concrete building on a busy corner in Shar e Naw, the district of Kabul where most of the foreign embassies and NGOs are based. Booking at the Mustafa is not necessary. It has numerous dusty, empty rooms accessed, as are the shared shower rooms, off open balconies around an internal court. There are bars everywhere. Every door and window in the hotel is barred – the office, the reception and kitchen, and the dining, sitting, and television rooms. Every vista the hotel offers is through bars. This confers a rather besieged, yet slightly absurd, atmosphere on the place. We later discover the hotel is like this because it was built to be a gold market. Then the Soviet Union invaded Afghanistan and the owners decided that running a hotel offered them a slightly better prospect than running a gold market. We choose a room on the top floor of the back building before sitting down to a lunch of meat balls, okra, and rice. Friday is the Muslim Sabbath, a relatively quiet day. After lunch we wander around the corner to Chicken Street, and scan the traditional crafts and souvenirs – Afghan hats and scarves, and kitsch synthetic tapestries bearing the portrait of Ahmed Shah Massoud, the charismatic Tajik Mujahedin leader killed by an Al Qaeda bomb just days before the Northern Alliance entered Kabul.

Saturday 12 10 02

While washing in the shower room we meet Steve Komarow, a journalist who writes for *USA Today*. He is going for a press briefing at Bagram, the American air base about an hour's drive from Kabul, which was originally built by the Russians. He offers us a ride in his jeep.

We take the 'new road' – built by the Russians in an attempt to forestall the constant ambushes they suffered in the villages on the 'old road'. The new road is empty except for the occasional check point manned by local Afghan militia.

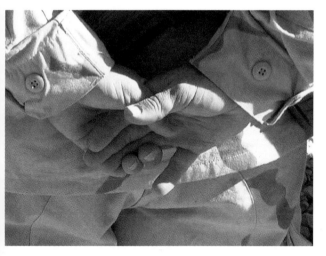

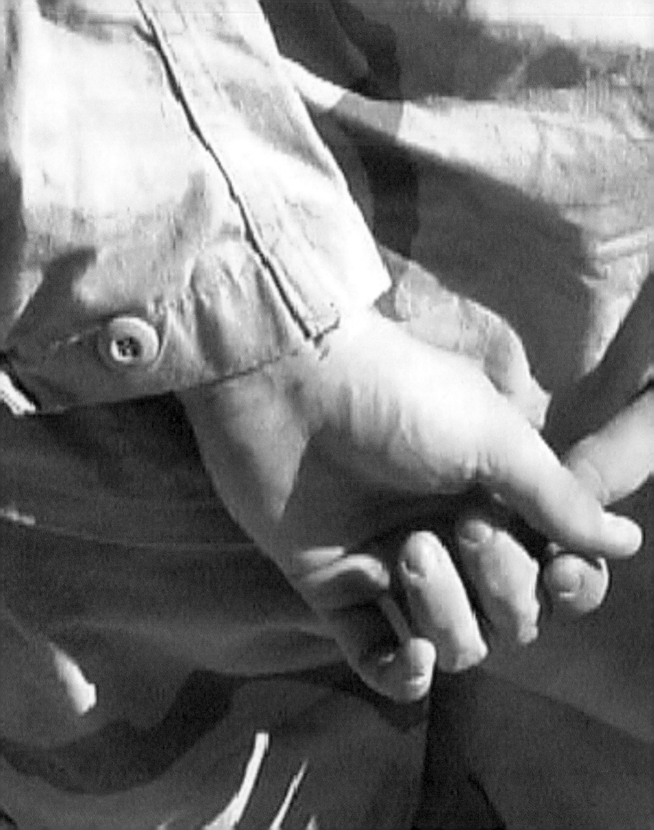

The entrance to Bagram Air Base is preceded by a ramshackle village, which has sprung up along side the road to cater to the passing traffic. It is surrounded by a sector controlled by the ANA (the embryonic multi-ethnic Afghan National Army). We are admitted through several checkpoints manned by well armed ANA troops, wearing an ad-hoc mixture of khaki and traditional Afghan dress (it is impossible for the new comer to tell initially which Afghan army, militia, or other para military group a given individual belongs to, but we are assured this is who they are). Finally we arrive at the heavily fortified gates to the American sector and wait for an escort from 'Media Ops'.

The press briefing takes place in the open air, and details the seizure of an illicit arsenal of prodigious size discovered in some warehouses outside the city of Kandahar. While the seemingly endless listing of the different types of munitions proceeds, there is a constant coming and going of American soldiers of different shapes, sizes, sexes, and ethnic backgrounds, all carrying arms despite their well protected position.

We ask permission to video the Boneyard, a vast scrap heap of assorted mainly Soviet made military aircraft dumped by the main runway. We drive out to it in a jeep, and are warned not to step off the hard standing, as there are land mines and other unexploded munitions lying around. Many of the aircraft have their Soviet air force insignia augmented with Afghan or Islamic signs and slogans, reflecting their subsequent service, during the civil war which ensued when the Russians pulled out, and then with the Taliban.

After collecting a gift of some self-heating MRE's (meals ready to eat), we leave the base and return to Kabul via the old road. We pass through ruined villages where the only complete houses left standing have heavy machine guns perched

on their roofs. Destroyed houses and compounds stand crumbling between ruined orchards, vineyards, and graveyards. The only surplus in this once fertile and productive agricultural region seems to be dust. The strange, wobbly hump-arsed sheep grazing among the abandoned tanks and military vehicles must eat dust. There appears to be nothing else.

The road, one of the very few paved roads in the whole country, is lined for miles on either side, with rows of rocks spaced about a metre apart. They are painted half white, and half bright red. The white sides face inward. The red sides face out to the land, indicating that we are in the middle of a minefield. Occasionally we pass men in overalls and heavy protective clothing crouching in the heat and dust at the roadside. They painstakingly check the ground, centimetre by centimetre, with a metal detector and a small hand trowel. Cars and lorries thunder by only inches away.

We pass some large Northern Alliance (predominantly Tajik) encampments surrounded by gun emplacements. As we approach Kabul, we slow down for the checkpoint on the city limits, under an enormous billboard of Ahmed Shah Massoud. Like Che's image in Cuba, Massoud's image is everywhere. In the valley in front of us, the capital disappears into the distance under a haze of smoke and dust which the sharp mountain sun illuminates from above, but cannot fully penetrate. There is a terrible smell and we pass the corpse of a man half-covered by a green shroud, lying in the road. It is crowded and people pass by apparently oblivious on either side. There are ramshackle brick kilns with huge stores of firewood, and a large cemetery on a slope. The green flags of the martyrs flutter from the graves in the bright sunlight.

After a quick lunch back at the Mustafa we go out to change some money in the gold market, and take photographs of hotel facades and entrances on the way. We wonder where the hotel owned by the Italian Arte Povera artist Alighiero e Boetti in the 1970's was, and if any evidence of it still remains. Afterwards we seek and find a place called CHA's Gallery of Fine Arts & Traditional Afghan Crafts. We are shown some recently made carpets using traditional techniques and natural dyes. They are exquisitely beautiful. CHA is a local NGO dedicated to preserving the tradition of Afghan carpet making, and promoting it abroad.

Sunday 13 10 02

At breakfast in the hotel we overhear an American couple in conversation with an Afghan woman dressed in western clothes and wearing a headscarf. They are enthusiastically discussing a girls' sewing school recently set up in the ruins nearby which they visited the previous day.

To support themselves and their families the girls are taught how to make clothes on old electric sewing machines. While half the group learn to sew on the machines, the other half pedal away on Chinese bicycles connected to a generator to provide the power. It is such a powerful image and sounds so resourceful to us that we ask the Afghan lady who took the academics, if we might also visit the school. She turns on us immediately, eyes flashing: "What

are you doing in Afghanistan?" she demands. We try to explain that we are researching a commission for the Imperial War Museum in London, about the aftermath of September 11th and the war in Afghanistan. "The Afghan people are fed up to death with researches and investigations. We need help, money! – not more investigations!" she declares, and walks straight out. The two American academics are as taken aback as we are by the vehemence of her response, and apologise to us after she leaves. We have already seen enough to think that what she said was entirely reasonable.

Despite all the loud promises of aid and assistance being made internationally, the Afghan people see little evidence of it on the ground. Partially as a result of this, the warlords are regaining their hold over the country because they appear to some people to offer the best options for employment, and individual advancement. A boy or a man can earn a dollar a day if they have their own assault rifle.

Still smarting from our encounter with the Sewing School mistress we visit the Red Cross HQ for a personal security briefing. The main tenets of the briefing are, watch where you tread at all times, stick to roads and paths which you know to be in use, do not find yourself outside after dark. On the way to the ICRC we spend some time taking photographs of the hand-painted signs outside the offices of the many NGOs based in the area. We are astonished at how many there are. When we ask, the ICRC is able to give us the definitive list of all the NGOs in Kabul (120 international NGOs and UN agencies alone). There are so many that one wonders what they are all doing. After the series of catastrophes which have befallen the country in the past twenty three years Afghanistan desperately needs all the help it can get in almost every field, but there are times when it starts to seem like the final revenge of the wealthy west. First you saturate the country with high-tech weaponry, then you bomb the place to bits, and finally when it's down on it's knees and completely flattened, you send in the NGOs in Timberland boots and brand new jeeps to rebuild it in your own image. As we leave the ICRC we come across a dog dying in an open drain. There doesn't seem to be an NGO for abandoned dogs yet but it may not be far off.

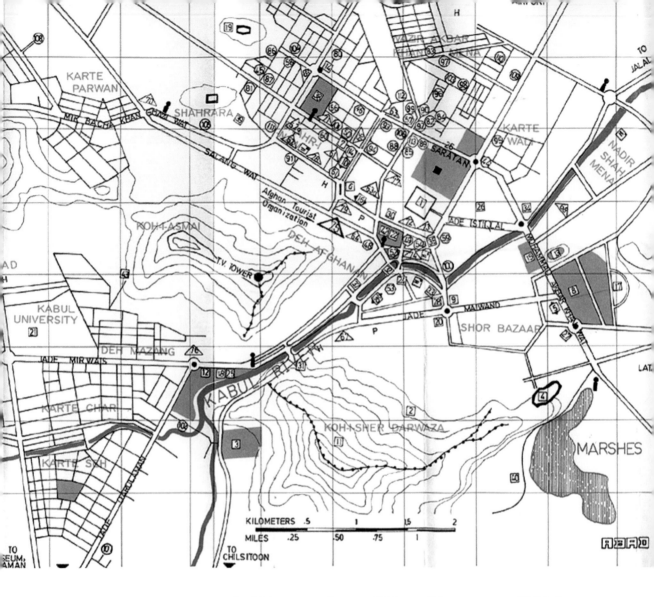

Next we go to the UN compound to see if it's possible to get on a UNHAS (UN Humanitarian Air Services) flight to Herat or Kandahar. After waiting for hours for someone who does not arrive, we are re redirected to the UN Travel Office, where we are told that the airport has been closed for security reasons. No one knows any more, just that there are no flights into or out of Kabul. At breakfast this morning we heard about the Bali bomb. We do not know if the two events are linked but it seems unlikely.

We decide to go and visit the British embassy instead, to let them know that we are in Kabul. We hail a taxi and try to find it, but we get hopelessly lost in the western suburbs of the city. There are no street names and few permanent landmarks left. For over twenty years, buildings, institutions, and even whole areas, have vanished, often overnight. This makes it difficult for people to get their bearings, and maps when available are of little use. It is rush hour now and everybody is trying to get home before dark and the curfew at six. Eventually we give up and retire to the hotel for dinner and to read, until a power cut plunges us into darkness.

Monday 14 10 02

Today we decide to visit the ISAF (International Security Force for Afghanistan) HQ. ISAF is the NATO derived multinational task force currently led by the Turks. ISAF only operates within Kabul. With the exception of Kandahar, where the US battle group hunting the Taliban and al Qaeda remnants is based, the rest of Afghanistan is still controlled entirely by warlords and their local commanders. This is why people everywhere derisively refer to the new Afghan President Hamid Karzai, as the "Mayor of Kabul". Most of the Afghan people, desperate for peace, would prefer a stable united country with a national army

drawn from all the ethnic groups. No one believes that Karzai would last for a minute without ISAF and the Americans.

The ISAF briefing is given by Major Gordon Mac-Kenzie. After finishing his account of mysterious night time explosions and abandoned corpses, he invites us to accompany him to camp Souter, the British base. The base is named after the last infantryman left standing, wrapped in the regimental colours, on the ill-fated British retreat from Kabul in 1842. It is in an old fertiliser factory built by the Soviets on the outskirts of the city in the 1970's. It is currently the largest construction site in Kabul. Army tents have been pitched inside the cavernous

concrete spaces of the factory. Under canvas under concrete, there are rows of bunks, and a busy canteen serving freshly prepared food to the British troops and roving groups of American special forces personnel fed up with the MRE's available at the US base. Running down the centre of the canteen tent between the dining tables, is a rough wooden gun rack accommodating an international array of automatic rifles and machine guns. Outside teams of Afghan construction workers in turbans and shalwar kameez are labouring enthusiastically under the direction of a Royal Engineers Officer called Iain Ogden to convert the camp into a permanent all weather base. As the Union flag flutters in the breeze above rising clouds of dust and smoke, we are served green tea on the roof.

Once tea is over we decide to go across the city to the Hotel Intercontinental to use Kabul's only internet cafe. The hotel is perched on a hill to the west of town and offers a 360 degree view over the whole city. Through the dust haze we can see the giant tent where the Loya Jirga was held, the Bala Hissar fortress, vacated to their cost by the British in 1870, and various Soviet era concrete apartment buildings rising charred and gaunt from the rubble of the city blocks. Tiny cars wind their way among the potholes, and as we look at the western suburbs reaching into the distance, Tahir our translator (an ethnic Pashtun) remarks that 50,000 people died below us in the civil war of the early 1990's, as Massoud's predominantly Tajik forces fought for control of the city. Despite this, but perhaps helped by the circumstances of his death, Massoud is now officially hailed in Kabul as a great leader of national liberation.

The Hotel Intercontinental was built by Taylor Woodrow in the late 1960s. It is a dusty and dilapidated period piece, where one can still decipher expectations of a future of international modernity and corporate sophistication that never arrived. Ceiling tiles hang loosely – in the lobby and the glass counters where one normally sees a banal display of Hermes scarves and sanitised local crafts contain only dust and a few earwigs. In the 'brasserie' one wall is covered by a large mural relief of the giant Buddhas at Bamyan. It is totally wrecked, with its Buddhas smashed by the Taliban in an absurd echo of the real event.

We get back in the car and decide to go to the British Embassy which we have ascertained is not far away. When we arrive the deputy head of mission meets us in the garden, asks politely what we are doing in Kabul, and informs us that Foreign Office advice is that travel to Afghanistan is not recommended. We

explain why we have come, and show him a book of our work. As we are about
to leave he bids us to follow him inside the embassy building, past a pair of
full length portraits of King Edward VII and Queen Alexandra, to see some old
black and white photos of an elegant neo classical mansion set in a luxuriant
garden. This he says, was the original British embassy. It was offered as a gift to
the newly created state of Pakistan at independence in 1947, and finally accepted
in 1975. He then bids us to follow him once more, and leads us out of the main
gate of the embassy compound, into the street, and straight through an equally
massive steel gate next door. We stand in a large unkempt garden, looking at
the same elegant house we have just seen in the black and white photographs
on the embassy wall. The white stucco is now smoke blackened, and there are
no doors or windows. The ground all around is littered with broken glass, and
fragments of burnt timber and crumbling plaster. Apparently when the city

of Herat in western Afghanistan fell to the Taliban in 1997, a mob of Kabulis realising that their city would be next, and incensed at the continuous support given to the Taliban by Pakistan, marched on the embassy and vented their anger and frustration by sacking it.

Finally we go to the Supreme Court of the Transitional Government of Afghanistan to see if we can obtain permission to attend a court case. Formal court proceedings are something of a novelty in Kabul, as all decision making processes whether civil, political, religious or military, became increasingly secluded, secretive, and seemingly arbitrary under Taliban rule. Tahir, our translator, becomes very excited as he tells us that we have been invited by the judge to attend an execution at the governor of Kabul's palace the next day.

Before returning to the hotel we decide to change some currency. On our way to the gold market, we stop and discretely take some photos of the bustling street in the evening rush hour. Suddenly we are gripped by a tiny girl dressed in rags. We look down as she pulls at our coats with one hand, while clenching a thick wad of Afghan notes in the other. Our moment of mild surprise at this incongruity is immediately superseded by horror as we see she has only half a face. The child's intent visage turns and collapses. There is nothing except a contorted slab of scars over smashed bone, and a residual void where once there was an eye. We give her some money, but nothing is enough, she won't let go. She pursues us everywhere, and no matter how we try, we cannot loose her. The thought of going into a gold brokers to change money becomes so crazy we retreat.

Tuesday 15 10 02

At the Governors palace the next day we realise that what we have been invited to is a murder trial, not an execution. While we wait for the trial to begin, we are introduced to a mullah who is a judge. He shakes hands with Nikki and laughs, saying that he never normally shakes hands with a woman. Sitting near to us is a group of young female trainee reporters making notes. Their teacher is a mature woman dressed in western clothes wearing a head scarf. Our translator whispers to us that she is a 'dog washer'. Astonished by his terminology, we ask what he means. It transpires that this is a term Afghans, who endured the

Russian occupation and the civil war, use for people who left the country at the time to work in the west, and who, in some cases, are now returning.

The court room in the palace compound fills with people who have journeyed from the countryside to attend. Suddenly the accused: Abdullah Shah, and his accomplice Mohammed Arif, enter the court in leg irons and handcuffs, accompanied by armed guards. Shah was a notorious commander during the civil war who served under another wanted commander called Zardad in the Hezb-i-Islami faction. He gained the title '███████████' for savaging travellers with his teeth before killing them, when collecting tolls on goods passing through Sarobi, a town midway between Kabul and Jalabad. The court falls silent as the two men make their way, shackles clanking, to their seats on the podium.

Before the trial commences, a middle aged man in traditional dress, with fair hair and a ruddy complexion, takes a seat beside the clerk, and sings out a prayer to bless the court. The prayer rises in the austere room, above the sound of the odd shuffle and cough, with a haunting beauty. The prosecutor reads out a list of charges which seems to go on for ever. Shah is accused of murdering dozens of people, including three of his own wives, by setting fire to them and throwing

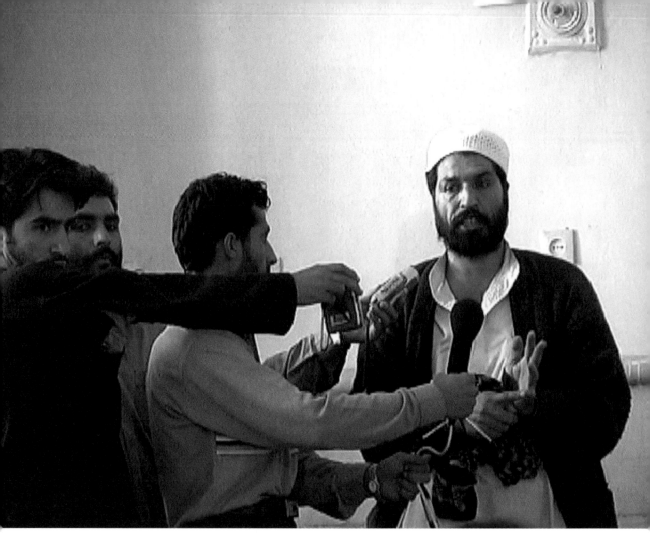

them into a well, and five of his own children – some of whom he butchered, cutting off their ears and noses. Shah has no defence counsel. He answers the charges himself by denying everything, dismissing all the evidence as gossip and hearsay, perpetrated by grudge-bearing neighbours. A long succession of witnesses takes the stand. Each of them gives their name and a thumb print to the clerk of the court before testifying. Most are very upset indeed. As each gives their evidence, struggling to control their grief, Shah sits behind them snarling and sneering, while his accomplice sits staring into space with a bored and gormless expression. We video the proceedings from our seat. The atmosphere is very tense but no one objects.

Finally the clerk of the court announces the verdict. He declares Shah guilty. The room suddenly erupts and the air convulses with cries of God Is Great!

When everyone in the room calms down Shah is sentenced to death by the judge. He responds by saying that these events took place during a time of war, and he was obliged by circumstances to act as he did. He will appeal. Islamic law allows for two further appeals, and the sentence has to be finally ratified by the president, Hamid Karzai. If Shah is executed, it will be the first death sentence to be enacted by the new government.

Postscript

On Tuesday 27th April 2004 the BBC reported that Abdullah Shah had been executed by a single bullet to the head in the Pul-e-Charki prison, Kabul, the previous week. His family were not informed of his execution at the time. After seeing his corpse, approximately three days after his death, his brother said his nose had been broken with what looked like a blow from a rifle butt.

Amnesty International commented, *Abdullah Shah was denied even basic standards of fairness, saying, execution may have been an attempt by powerful political players to eliminate a key witness to human rights abuses.*

The office of Hamid Karzai the president of Afghanistan, commented, *the president felt compelled by the need to ensure justice to the victims.*

In April 2003 Faryadi Sarwar Zardad *Commander Zardad* was discovered living in Streatham, south London. He was running a Pizza restaurant in nearby Bexleyheath. He had fled the Taliban in 1996 and made his way to Britain in 1999. Zardad was arrested on charges of torture and hostage taking, and held in Belmarsh Prison in south east London. On Friday 8th October 2004 he came to trial at the High Court at the Old Bailey. At the time of preparing this book for publication the trial is in progress and expected to last 8–10 weeks.

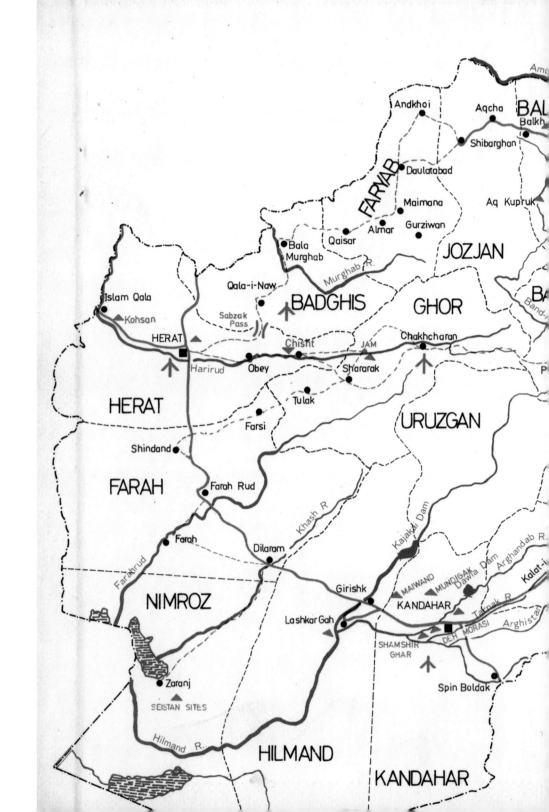

Andkhoi

Aqcha

BAL

Balkh

FARYAB

Shibarghan

Daulatabad

Maimana

Aq Kupruk

JOZJAN

Almar   Gurziwan

Bala   Qaisar

Murghab

Murghab R.

BA

Band-

Qala-i-Naw

Islam Qala

Kohsan

BADGHIS   GHOR

Sabzak
Pass

Chakhcharan

HERAT

Chisht

JAM

Harirud   Obey

Shararak

Tulak

URUZGAN

Farsi

HERAT

Shindand

FARAH

Farah Rud

Khash R

Kajaki Dam

Farahrud

Farah

Dilaram

Girishk

MAIWAND   MUNDIGAK   Dahla Dam   Arghandab R.

Kalat-i

KANDAHAR   Tarnak R.

NIMROZ

Lashkar Gah

DEH MORASI   Arghistan

SHAMSHIR
GHAR

Zaranj

SEISTAN SITES

Spin Boldak

Hilmand R.

HILMAND

KANDAHAR

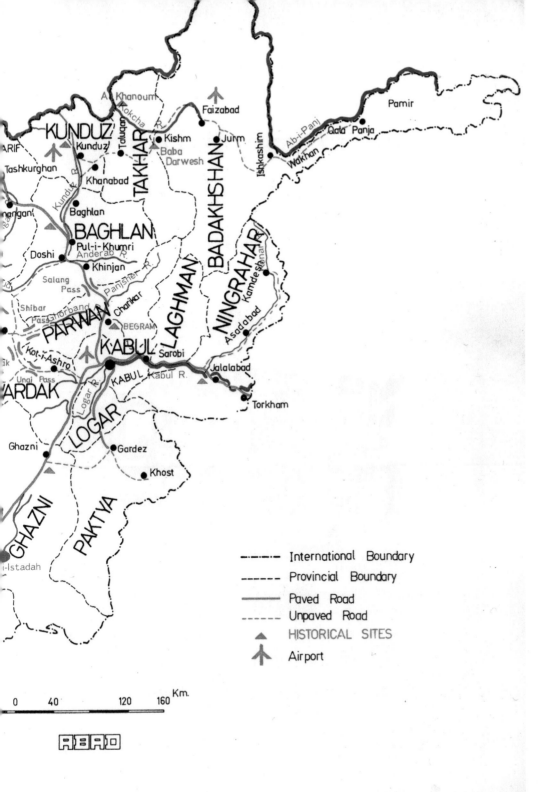

International Boundary
Provincial Boundary
Paved Road
Unpaved Road
HISTORICAL SITES
Airport

0   40   120   160   Km.

After the court case ends we visit the UN Compound to see Jim Williams. As senior project specialist at UNESCO, Jim is concerned with co-ordinating international efforts towards the reconstruction of the destroyed Buddhas of Bamyan. In his office we see an artist's impression of how the monumental Buddhas might appear after reconstruction which makes them look like sculptures by Anthony Gormley. We ask Jim's advice about travelling to Bamyan and Jalabad. He tells us that the road to Bamyan is considered safe, but the road to Jalabad is too dangerous. Two vehicles have been rocketed at Sarobi in the last couple

of days. There have been many other attacks in the same area, one of the most notorious being the murder of four journalists in November 2001. Jim also confirms that the airport remains closed. The reason is because a local militia group have dug up an undisclosed cache of Stinger missiles, and are reluctant to hand them over. They are resaleable and potentially very valuable. There is a stand off and until the negotiations are concluded there will be no flights. The Stinger is the weapon that finally broke the will of the Russians to remain in Afghanistan: it is so lethally effective in bringing down aircraft.

Wednesday 16 10 02

We are offered eggs for breakfast: fried, boiled, scrambled, or omelette? We opt for scrambled and are brought omelette, again. We change money at the gold market. As we pack our rucksack with the brick sized bundles of notes the currency dealer invites us to take tea with him. This is the first time we have ever been offered tea by a Bureau de Change. Maybe they could try this at Gatwick.

We look for and finally hire a 4x4 to take us to Bamyan the next day. Negotiations concluded, we have a lunch of Ashak (Afghan spinach dumplings) which proves to be the best thing we have eaten during our trip so far.

We then go on to the Kabul Museum at Dar ul Aman, to meet Mr Omarakhan Masoodi, the director. He is an absolutely charming man sitting in a bare office covered in dust. As we interview him he tells us the heartbreaking story of the devastation wrought on the museum and its collection during the civil war, and subsequently by the Taliban. He also recounts the ingenious ruses he and his staff deployed to protect from destruction the 30% of the collection that survives, and he tells us about the promises of help and money emanating from the West, that never materialise.

The area of Dar ul Aman where the museum is situated, is centred on the bombed out Royal Palace, which was finally devastated by American cruise missiles when the Taliban refused to surrender Osama Bin Laden after September 11th. Once upon a time Dar ul Aman was an extremely wealthy area, inhabited by the aristocracy, and the very rich. They built themselves grand villas set in gracious gardens. Everything is now in ruins. Numerous gutted palaces stand fragmenting in a bleak desert of dust, rubble, and rusting munitions. The beguiling irony is that, leaving aside the human cost of the destruction, the kitsch neoclassicism of the architecture is much improved by its current condition.

Thursday 17 10 02

We rise at 4.30 am to travel to Bamyan as soon as the curfew lifts. At 5 am we leave Kabul by the road to Gazni. There are no street lights or light of any other kind, except for the headlights of our 4x4 picking out a path of dust into the blackness. It is a world of complete darkness and cold. Occasionally men and donkeys carting piles of firewood towards the city loom into view. Bent double, straining against their loads, their eyes reflect darkly back at us. We pass through Maidan Shah and turn off the paved road onto a rutted dusty track, which follows a river through numerous Pashtun villages. The land along the river bank has been intensively cultivated with numerous tiny, tidy, empty fields. The harvest has been recently gathered.

By mid morning we are deep in the mountains. We pass through a military checkpoint manned by Hazara militia on a deserted road, and stop for breakfast at the next village we come to. The tea house consists of one large carpeted room with men and boys sitting in small groups against the walls on grubby cushions and folded quilts. We take off our shoes and sit on some spare quilts below a window, and find that the floor is pleasantly warm. The teahouse doubles as an inn at night and has under floor heating provided by a fire outside at the back. This is a practical comfort in this region, as the nights can be bitterly cold. A boy comes over and greets us pleasantly, before unrolling what looks like a vinyl stair mat on the floor in front of us. A host of flies immediately land on the mat before being briefly dispersed by a brisk wipe from a cloth shiny black with grime. His shalwar kameez is also so solid with encrusted grime that in parts the cotton fabric more resembles oilskin. The window above our heads

swings open and four steaming nan like breads, each two feet long, are slapped down on the 'stair mat' in front of us. The bread is dustily fragrant with toasted flour and absolutely delicious. It is accompanied by kebabs of liver, and a dish of eggs sizzling in oil.

The route from here on becomes more and more mountainous. Our four-wheel drive struggles to negotiate the ruts and crags of a barely discernible road, which more closely resembles the blasting area of a quarry. Eventually we rise over the Hajigak pass at 12,140 feet, and begin our descent in the direction of Bamyan. In places the land becomes a little greener. Tiny farms line each valley bottom with everybody out collecting the harvest. Farmers walk oxen and donkeys around in circles on stone threshing floors in the open air. Boys in woollen hats and women in bright reds, blues, and greens, toss fork fulls of wheat in the wind to winnow the grain. Unlike the Pashtun women who wear the all-covering burkha in a single colour, the Hazara women wear long dresses and scarves of many colours. Children crouch in the sun, gleaning the fields, or tending the cattle and sheep grazing on the steep slopes.

Following the ever present river down through the narrow Pai Mori gorge, we pass a hot spring beside the road. The rock around the pool is tinted vivid orange and red by the minerals dissolved in the water. We pass above some beautiful qala (traditional courtyard houses) with pyramid piles of wheat on the roofs, and emerge into a wide valley bordered by a vast red mountain. Set into the cliffs are the crenelated forms of the Shar-i-Zohak, the 'Red Fort' reputedly built by Genghis Khan, which signals the beginning of the Bamyan valley.

By comparison with most other areas we have seen so far, the valley floor is quite green. As in other places in Afghanistan, poplar trees have been planted in place of the original species, because they are quick growing. At least there are trees. Most other areas of the country still suffer terrible de-forestation, which has seriously exacerbated the five-year drought.

Suddenly at a distance we spot the caves and the enormous parabolic voids where the Buddhas once stood. We approach another checkpoint manned by Hazara Militia, indicated by a row of spent artillery shell cases, standing upright like bollards in the dust. We pass under a banner declaring 'Welcome to Bamyan', and enter the town, which consists of a single muddy street lined with shacks and kiosks, hastily constructed out of a variety of salvaged building materials supported on mud bricks. Malik, our translator, says we should head straight for the 'famous restaurant', which turns out to be the only restaurant in Bamyan.

On our way in, we step over a dead goat which has been skinned and then abandoned. The distended red and blue carcass covered with skeins of opalescent fat lies glistening in the dust. As we enter the tea house there is another skinned carcass dangling in the doorway. The cook is vigorously removing choice sections using a bare blade with no handle. We push past more carcasses hanging in the corri-

dor (there is no refrigeration), to enter the tea room and sit down. Everybody is eagerly watching an Indian film. The story of a swashbuckling hero leaping energetically from crag to crag through silk flags, and cutting down his opponents with a flashing sabre on the way, seems not at all out of place. The room smells warmly of unwashed bodies. We are brought tea, and not really fancying flesh this time, we order a bowl of rice, which turns out to be tepid and still have small pieces of fatty meat lurking below the surface. The bread is cold and stale. Sensibly as it turns out, Malik and Akbar stick to kebabs. Reluctant to offend our companions or fellow patrons in the teahouse, we force ourselves to eat a few mouthfuls of the rice, but soon have to give up. After lunch we are shown the sleeping quarters: one enormous room above the room we have been eating in. There are enough of the folded quilts to accommodate about thirty people. The toilet, which you can smell before you see it, is down a ladder and two hundred yards away. It seems to be the only toilet in the town. The ground around about is festooned with deposits left by people who never made it inside. Fortunately we have heard that there is a UN guest house a few miles away, and we are relieved to find that they have a room.

The Bamyan valley is beautiful. It is broad and long, and being enclosed entirely by mountains, it has the air of a secret kingdom. The towering cliffs, pierced by numerous caves, glow rich bronze in the afternoon sun. We make our way on dust roads across the valley floor towards 'the Big Buddha'. All that remains is the cavity in the cliff. This in itself is over 180 feet high and still impressive. The towering hollow is riven with cracks and littered at its base with an enormous

pile of shattered boulders. A charming young teenager with almost Japanese features, and a rifle slung over his shoulder, paces up and down, standing guard over the rubble and the cave chambers, to prevent further looting. Looking back across the valley we see the remains of the old town of Bamyan, destroyed by the Taliban. An arcade of collapsing arches beside the road, was once a row of shops. A few broken walls stand adjacent, daubed loosely with white painted letters and numbers, arrows and dotted lines, HT 23 _ _ > , the insignia and codes of the Halo Trust, one of the mine clearance teams, indicates that recovery has begun. As it must. No reconstruction can begin until the lethal explosives waiting in the ground, are exposed and removed. We film and take photographs. It is strangely peaceful. In the distance three men wrapped in woollen cloaks against the cold sit on a large rock overlooking the valley.

The sun is starting to set and the cliffs are a blazing gold. We decide to make our way along the valley edge to the Small Buddha. Sitting huddled on the ground in front of a grave are three little girls. None of them is more than eight

years old. They are dressed in bright red, pink, and green, and wrapped against the cool of the evening in long scarves of similar colours. They giggle and hide their faces as we approach. Above them sit two of their brothers watching. Washing is laid out on the rocky slope to dry. As we are walking back to the jeep, a boy of about fourteen tentatively approaches us. Malik tells us he is the head of the family who live in the cave above us. We climb up over a steep scree. Outside the entrance to the cave, a pressure cooker is hissing away on a fire made of a few sticks, its smoke curling upwards. A makeshift ladder leads up to an inner recess. The ceiling of the cave is carved and deeply coffered, with a rigorous geometric design based on a rotated square on a circle. The ancient frescoes which once covered the boldly incised pattern, have long been obliterated by soot. Many people have moved into the caves. The town of Bamyan was destroyed by the Taliban and little of it has been rebuilt. They have nowhere else to go, and with the coming winter the caves are warmer at night than tents (which are sometimes available from the UN agencies).

We return across the valley to the UN guest house to sleep. Seated on the floor at dinner, we meet an ex-New Zealand special forces soldier, who is working with a Danish de-mining group. He has been everywhere in the world disposing of live munitions and removing mines. Cambodia, Angola, the Balkans, the Iran-Iraq border. We ask him which is the worst place. Unhesitatingly he says Afghanistan. He finishes by telling us that even if another mine is never laid on earth, it will still take a thousand years at the present rate of clearance, to make the world safe. In Afghanistan somebody is blown to bits by a mine every hour of the day.

Friday 18 10 02

The next morning we rise in the cold pitch black. In the early sunlight of the dawn we resume our exploration of the caves. Many are surprisingly warm within, the rock having retained heat from the previous days sun during the night. All the ancient Buddhist frescoes we come across are badly defaced by looters, smoke or vandals. Live and spent ammunition litters the ground almost everywhere. At 10am it is time to leave, or we will not make it back to Kabul

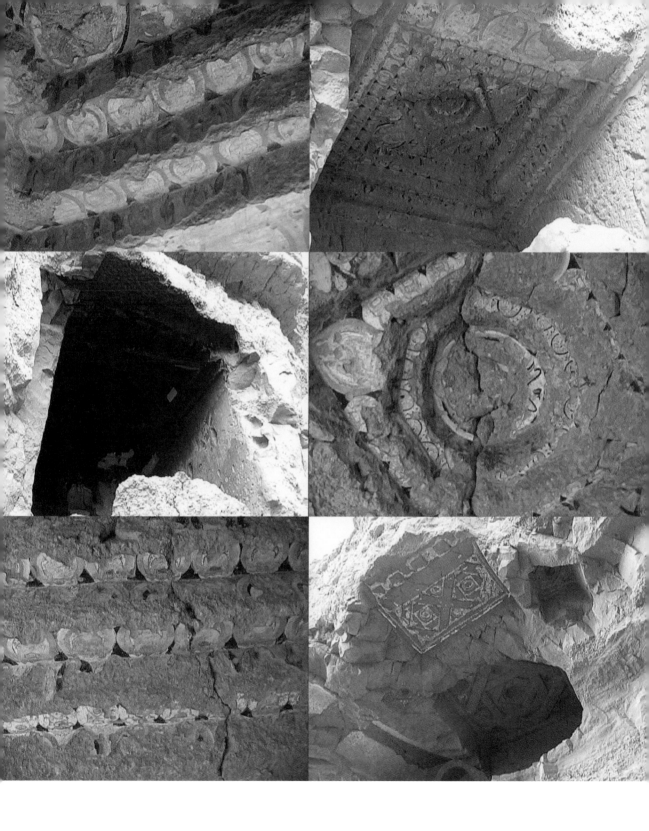

before the curfew. We take the road over the Shibar pass. Soon we are completely covered in dust. We keep the windows of the four-wheel drive tightly closed, but it comes up through the floor and gets everywhere including our camera equipment, despite it being sealed inside plastic bags when not in use. The landscape is severe with a biblical simplicity. We pass through villages of mud brick houses with piles of dung stacked neatly on every roof to dry, there being no other fuel. We arrive in a village with numerous stalls selling sacks of red onions. Half way down the single main street is a Russian tank literally stopped dead in its tracks. Stalls have been built up to and around it as though it were a rock or some other immovable feature of the landscape. Everything of any usable value has been stripped off it, leaving just its bulky hollow carcass, too heavy and disabled to shift. We stop and buy the most delicious dried mulberries and almonds from a roadside vendor before continuing. Four hours into the journey Nikki starts to suffer badly from stomach cramps but there is little we can do. We can't even stop for a discrete toilet break as we are surrounded by mine fields, and it is too dangerous to leave the road, with its intermittent but continuous traffic of people walking, on donkeys, or in heaving jeeps and lorries. Eventually as darkness starts to fall the number of people on the road decreases substantially. We are in a completely deserted and rocky valley. Lines of painted rocks indicating the presence of mines run in every direction. Malik our translator, and Akbar our driver, begin to get slightly nervous at our lack of progress, and try to speed up, but the road is so bad it is impossible. This makes us nervous. Finally we pass a militia post in the darkness, and re-join the pot-holed but paved road into Kabul.

Saturday 19 10 02

At breakfast, Steve invites us to join him on a trip to Jebel Saraj, followed by
Bagram Air Base, to see General Franks, who is on a flying visit to the troops.
Jebel Saraj was the Northern Alliances base for the assault on Kabul, as well as
the HQ of the international media. However Steve wants to write a piece for
USA Today about some duck decoys he saw on a lake there once and also visit
a knife seller nearby. On arriving at Jebel Saraj, we climb over a wall and run
down a dusty track, to find about eight very realistic decoy ducks sitting
peacefully on the water. The local carpenter arrives with an axe, and offers to
make Steve his own decoy as a souvenir. This takes him about ten minutes. As
he works using some pieces of poplar wood which are lying nearby, the owner
of the decoys arrives with his rifle. He decides that we should also have one
from the lake and jumps straight into the freezing water to get it. This show
of instant bravura in the cold water turns out to be an irresistible sales pitch,
and negotiations for the two decoys together conclude at twelve dollars. This
is a very good sum when one considers that economics are so distorted in
Afghanistan that a doctor or teacher in Kabul can only expect to earn around
thirty dollars a month, while a driver working for an NGO or a gunman can
earn considerably more.

When we arrive at the Bagram Air Base the US troops are gathering in the compound to practice their parade in honour of General Franks. Tommy Franks is the general in charge of *Centcom* (Central Command), one of the five areas of command into which the Pentagon has divided the world. In time-honoured American fashion, Franks' foreign touring schedule is intense, and he might soon be even busier. Apart from including Afghanistan, Centcom also includes Iraq. Franks is a 'soldiers' soldier, and is known for voicing his opinion that military plans seldom survive first contact with the enemy.

Eventually, the plane with Franks on board, touches down and the parade begins. It is an informal event in comparison with the British Army's equivalent. Before long Franks, escorted by his Special Forces minders, is mingling with his troops, slapping each of them on the back, and posing for photographs with his arms around their shoulders.

Sunday 20 10 02

We spend the morning in Kabul taking photographs in the street, and waiting around in offices for people who never arrive. In the afternoon we return to take photographs at the burnt out Pakistani Embassy. At our hotel in the evening we see the aftermath of a terrorist bomb in the Philippines on the satellite television.

Monday 21 10 02

We rise at 4 am intending to get a good start on the road to Jalabad. We have been told we have a five and half hour drive to our destination in front of us, and we have to return to Kabul before dark the same day. Suddenly Waiz the hotel owner emerges, torch in hand from his barred room, insisting that it is too early and too dangerous to leave the building. As soon as he goes back to bed, we persuade the doormen sleeping downstairs to open up and let us out. We get into the jeep and set off along the deserted roads in the dark. At the border of the district of Kabul, we are stopped by some ANA soldiers who at first refuse to let us pass. After scrutinising our passports for so long that we fear they might not be returned to us, they are finally persuaded that we are foreigners, and we can proceed. We do not understand the logic in this, but we don't question it.

We leave the plateau of Kabul and enter the top of the Tangi Gharu Gorge. It is still dark but we can see that the road twists and turns dramatically downwards, because it is lined with lorries, headlights on in the dark, making their way slowly upwards to join the queue of lorries waiting to enter the capital.

As dawn breaks we find ourselves in some of the bleakest terrain we have so far encountered. This is despite the fact that we are on one of the most important roads in the whole country, and the main artery by which the city of Kabul is supplied. Our jeep heaves and grinds its way among the boulders, raising clouds of dust as it goes. Eventually the gorge widens into a valley and we reach the town of Sarobi. The name 'Sarobi' chills the blood of westerners in Afghanistan, since four western journalists passing through the town in November 2001 were stopped, hauled out of the vehicle in which they were travelling, and shot

dead. A wide area surrounding the town is controlled by a notoriously ruthless commander called Hazarat Ali, who is allied to Gulbuddin Hekmatyar, leader of the ultra conservative Hezb-i-Islami, and one of the most powerful warlords in Afghanistan. Hekmatyar was one of the main beneficiaries of finance and support directed through Pakistan during the Russian occupation, and the civil war which followed it. Like many of the Afghan warlords and commanders, he found his power severely curtailed during the Taliban period. Now that the Taliban have gone, and flush with American weaponry and a slice of the 70 million dollars handed out to the warlords by the CIA to buy their support, he is re-establishing his position in the area. With a private army of thousands of heavily armed men (most of whom will have changed sides at least once recently to work for whoever is most powerful in the area at the time), he controls a 'business' empire incorporating every significant source of income in the region – most of them highly illegal.

We pass quickly through the town and continue on our way through the Tangi Abreshom Gorge (The Silk Gorge), accompanied by the Kabul river. After passing many villages and qala (traditional fortified houses) the landscape opens out into a dry stony plain. Occasionally we see encampments of Kuchis, nomads, in very worn but richly decorated clothes. Their camels and flocks of sheep and goats, some of whom are also decorated with coloured braids, spread into the distance searching for grazing. Not surprisingly the number of Kuchis following the traditional way of life has declined dramatically in recent times.

The dry plain gives onto a wide sparsely cultivated valley, ringed by high mountains, which finally becomes the shallow muddy lake of the Darunta reservoir. The water level is very low. Here there are more frequent camps of Kuchis. We pass through the small village of Daruntah. Rounding a bend in the road just outside, we come to a check point manned by a gang of local Hezb-i-Islami militia. The boys are sitting under a shade of rush thatch on the roof of a small ruined house, with a machine gun on a tripod, guarding a turning off the road. We think this is likely to be the entrance to the house we are looking for. A house that was previously occupied by Osama Bin Laden. We pull up, and Malik asks if we may visit the house. They say that we may, but we need to pay a 'security fee' and take one of them with us or the rest of their unit in the house not knowing who we are, might shoot at us without warning. The sum required is 50,000 Afs or 1 US dollar. One of the boys picks up a Kalashnikov and climbs silently into the front of a jeep beside Malik and Akbar. We drive down the track and around a bend, passing under another machine gun post. It's unmanned this time, although the gun has a belt of bullets in it. We pull up in a compound below a house with a smashed mobile rocket launcher listing in front of it. A group of young men armed with assault rifles emerges from the house, followed by a commander who is probably in his late twenties or early thirties but so marked by experience that he could be almost any age. The men are quite matter of fact with us, neither friendly or unfriendly, which feels slightly unusual. Up until now all the Afghans we have met have been quite communicative people. We explain that we are interested in taking some

photos of the house and its surroundings. They ask us why we want the photos, but when we explain that we are researching a commission for a museum in London, they loose interest in our reason and tell us to go ahead.

The location of the house is quite spectacular. It is on a promontory projecting into the lake surrounded by tall mountains. It commands a panoramic 360-degree view of its surroundings. The compound comprises a series of ruins with several intact structures standing in an area of rough ground littered with discarded live munitions, abandoned military vehicles and rusting hardware. A full pallet of rockets for the mobile launcher stands in the sun with their cellophane wrapping from the factory still intact. The compound's principal building is a modest three-roomed house in the local vernacular style with a small terrace and an external

kitchen. This appears to be the oldest structure, and was probably originally built as a farmhouse. There is also a small mosque overlooking the house, and a strange bomb shelter/bunker behind it. The men tell us that these last two buildings were added by Bin Laden for his own use. The mosque is conventionally constructed out of local stone and rendered concrete, but the bunker is rather unusual. It is partially excavated and set into the ground. The walls are made from stacked wooden ammunition boxes filled with rocks and earth as ballast. It has an earth and stone roof set on branches over old Soviet lorry chassis. The whole is topped off with some old tyres. Bin Laden took up residence in the house when he moved to Afghanistan from Sudan in May 1996. After setting up a training camp for Jihadis he stayed until September 1997 when the activity of American agents in nearby Peshawar, Pakistan, induced him to seek greater safety in Kandahar. In 1998 when Al Qaida bombed the US embassies in Kenya and Tanzania the site was attacked with cruise missiles. On 9 October 2001 when the Taliban refused to surrender Bin Laden the site was again bombed by American B52s. While we are taking photographs, a pair of American Black Hawk helicopters appear from behind the mountains and pass low overhead. After they pass we decide to take some measurements of the house for future reference. As soon as we get our tape measure out and start making notes the fighters become agitated exclaiming, 'You asked to take photos why do you want this (the dimensions) as well?'. Our attempts to diffuse the tension by explaining that we might want to make a digital reconstruction of the house when we get back to London clearly make no sense at all in this situation and we decide it is best to leave.

Ben Langlands and Nikki Bell 2002

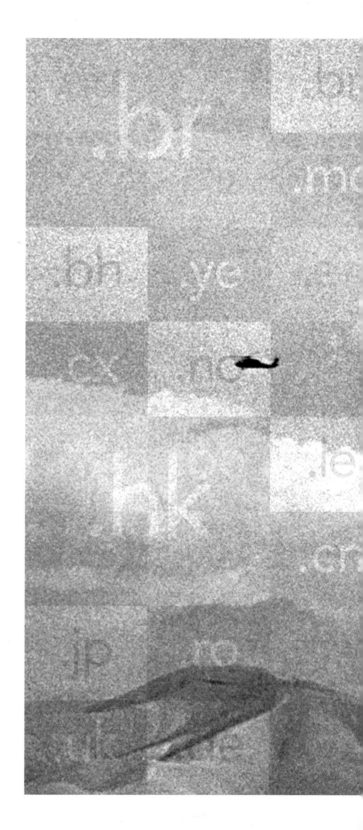

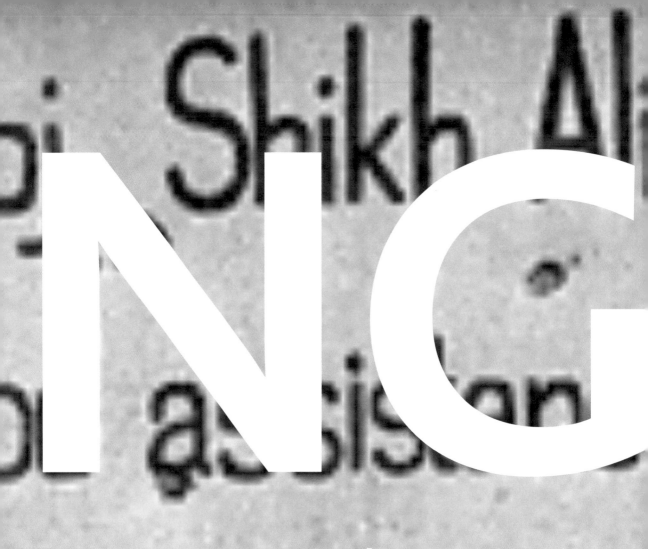

NG

Non Governmental Organisations

In October 2002 Langlands & Bell visited Afghanistan for a research commission awarded by the Art Commisions Committee of the Imperial War Museum in London titled: *The Aftermath of September 11 and The War in Afghanistan*.

Arriving in Afghanistan in October 2002 Langlands & Bell were immediately struck by the large number of NGOs, and UN and other donor agencies, operating in the country. At the time there were approximately 120 international NGOs and UN agencies, and 160 local Afghan NGOs, based in Kabul alone. The *aid community*, amounts to a global billion dollar industry which parallels and interconnects with the networks of global politics, commerce, and communications.

Langlands & Bell took numerous photographs of the signs the aid organisations had placed throughout the country to advertise their presence. These images were subsequently collated by the artists as part of the work.

In addition to the photos of the NGO signs Langlands & Bell made an animated mini movie using the codes and acronyms these bodies employ to identify themselves, *UNO, USAID, WFP, MDM, ICRC, United Nations Organisation, US Agency for International Development, World Food Programme, Médecins du Monde, International Committee of the Red Cross*, etc. in a series of graphic templates. The codes multiply, transform, and dissolve into each other in an infinite film loop which repeats every 8 minutes. The film illuminates the great number of these organisations which now exist and simultaneously alludes to the variety and pervasive range of their activities.

Langlands & Bell 2003

International NGOs and UN Agencies based in Kabul

AAA	Action Aid Afghanistan
AAD	Afghan Aid Development
ACBAR	Agency Coordinating Body for Afghan Relief
ACF	Action Contre la Faim
ACTED	Agence d'aide à la coopération technique et au dévelopment
ADRA	Adventist Development & Relief Agency
ADSI	Action & Dévelopment Solidaires International
AED	Academy for Educational Development
AFRANE	Amité Franco–Afghane
AIMS	Afghanistan Information Management Service (United Nations)
ALA	Afghanistan Libre Association
AMI	Aide Médicale Internationale
AMURT	Ananda Marga Universal Relief Team (Switzerland)
ATCE	Afghan-Turk Cag Educational
ATLAS	Action Transport Logistique Assistance Service
BRAC	Bangladesh Rural Advancement Committee
CARE	Coordination of Afghan Relief
CDAP	Comprehensive Disabled Afghans Programme (United Nations)
CFA	Child Fund Afghanistan
CHF	Community, Habitat, Finance
CIC	Children in Crisis
COOPI	Cooperazione Internazionale (Italy)
CORD AID	Cord Aid (Netherlands)
COW	Children of War

118

CPHA	Chak-e-Wardak Hospital Project
CRF	Canadian Relief Foundation
CRS	Catholic Relief Services
CWS	Church World Service
DACAAR	Danish Committee for Aid to Afghan Refugees
DCA	Dutch Committee for Afghanistan
DDG	Danish De-mining Group
DFID	Department for International Development
DWHH/GAA	Deutsche Welthungerhilfe/German Agro Action
EA	Euro Aid
ECHO	European Commission Humanitarian Aid Office
EFCR	European Foundation for Conflict Resolution
EMDH	Enfants du Monde Droits de l'Homme, les Droits de l'Enfant
EMERGENCY	Life Support for Civilian War Victims
FAO	Food and Agriculture Organisation (United Nations)
FOCUS	Focus on the Global South
GMS	German Medical Services
GNI	Good Neighbours International
GOAL	Goal International
GTZ	Deutsche Gesellschaft für Technische Zusammenarbeit
HEP	Help & Education Projects International Canada
HF	Hammer Forum
HHI	Habitat for Humanity International
HI(B)	Handicap International (Belgium)
HI(F)	Handicap International (France)
HOPE	Worldwide Hope
HNI	Health Net International

HRW	Human Rights Watch
IAM	International Assistance Mission
IBC	International Blue Crescent
ICMC	International Catholic Migration Commission
ICRC	International Committee of the Red Cross
IFES	International Foundation For Election Systems
IF HOPE	International Foundation of Hope
IFRC	International Federation of the Red Cross & Red Crescent
IHRLG	International Human Rights Law Group
IHSF	International Health Services Foundation
ILO	International Labour Organisation
IMC	International Medical Corps
INTERSOS	Intersos (Italy)
IOM	International Organisation for Migration
IR	Islamic Relief UK
IRC	International Rescue Committee
ISRA	Islamic Relief Agency
IUCN	The World Conservation Union
JCCP	Japan Center for Conflict Prevention
JEN	Japan Emergency NGO
KA	Kindershilfwerk Afghanistan e.V.
KfW	Kreditanstalt für Wiederaufbau
MADERA	Madera (BIA - Bureau International pour l'Afghanistan)
MDM	Médecins Du Monde
ME	Mission East
MEDICA	Medica Mondial

MERCY	Mercy Corps
MERLIN	Medical Relief International
MMCC	Mobile Mini Circus for Children
MRCA	Medial Refresher Courses for Afghans
MSF	Médecins Sans Frontières
MSH	Management Sciences for Health
NAC	Norwegian Afghanistan Committee
NCA	Norwegian Church Aid
OFARIN	Organisation zur Förderung Afghanischer Regionaler Initiativen
OI	Ockenden International
OMAR	Organisation for Mine Clearance & Afghan Rehabilitation
PARSA	Physiotherapy Therapy & Rehabilitation Support for Afghanistan
PHO	Polish Humanitarian Organisation
PWJ	Peace Winds Japan
RI	Relief International
SAB	Solidarité Afghanistan Belgium
SC	Save the Children
SCA	Swedish Committee for Afghanistan
SCJ	Save the Children - Japan
SCS	Save the Children - Sweden
SCUS	Save the Children - USA
SC UK	Save the Children - UK
SDC	Swiss Agency for Development and Cooperation
SERVE	Serving Emergency Relief & Vocational Enterprises
SFL	Shelter for Life International
SGAA	Sandy Gall's Afghanistan Appeal
SNI	Shaelet Now International
SOLIDARITES	Aide Humanitaire d'Urgence
SORA	Support Organisation for Refugees of Afghanistan

SWISS PEACE	Afghan Civil Society Forum
TEAR FUND	Tear Fund Disaster Response Team
TDH	Terre Des Hommes
TODAI	Relief Organisation in Japan
UCL	Leonard Cheshire Centre of Conflict Recovery
UMCOR	United Methodist Committee on Relief
UNAMA	United Nations Assistance Mission in Afghanistan
UNCHS	United Nations Commission for Human Settlement
UNDCP	United Nations Drug Control Programme
UNDP	United Nations Development Programme
UNESCO	United Nations Educational, Scientific and Cultural Organisation
UNFPA	United Nations Famiily and Population Agency
UNHCR	United Nations High Commissioner for Refugees
UNICA	United Nations International Committee for Afghanistan
UNICEF	United Nations International Childrens Emergency Fund
UNMSA	United Nations Special Mission to Afghanistan
UNOCHA	United Nations Office for Coordination of Humanitarian Affairs
UNOCHA/RMAC	United Nations Regional Mine Action Centre
UNOPS	United Nations Office for Project Services
USAID	US Agency for International Development
WFP	World Food Programme (United Nations)
WHO	World Health Organisation (United Nations)
WIN	World in Need
WORLD VISION	World Vision International Christian Relief
ZOA	Zust Oust Asia
ZUFLUCHT	Revolution One (Switzerland)

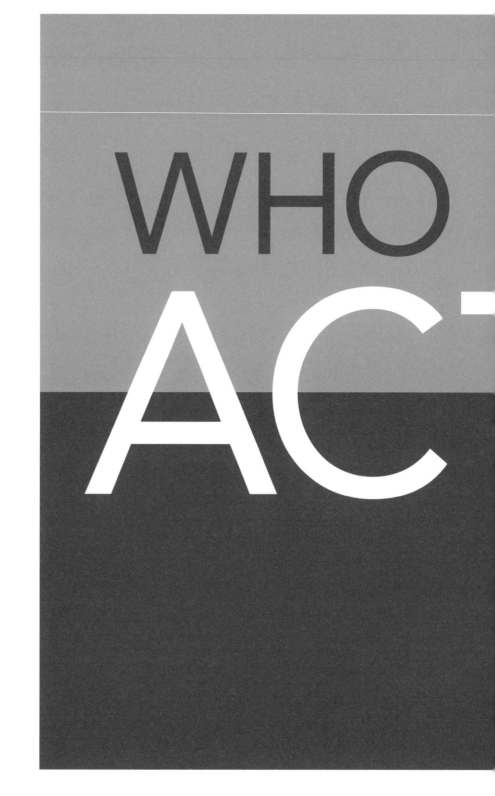

ED
CARE

Caught in the Crossfire

On 16 November 2003, Bettina Goislard, a 29 year-old French Protection Officer for the United Nations High Commissioner for Refugees (UNHCR), was shot dead as she drove through Ghazni, a town in south-eastern Afghanistan. Two gunmen on a motorbike drove up beside her vehicle and shot her six times in the chest at point blank range.

Two months before this attack, five Afghan staff of a Danish aid organisation were taken from their car, roped together with their hands behind their backs, and gunned down on the roadside. One survived, by pretending to be dead, and was later cut free from the corpses of his former colleagues. He said that the attackers told them the shootings were a reprisal for the treatment of detainees in Guantánamo Bay, just before they opened fire.

Over the course of the next 12 months around 40 more UN, humanitarian aid and reconstruction workers were murdered in Afghanistan. Virtually every humanitarian organisation has had its staff or offices threatened or attacked. In June 2004 *Médecins Sans Frontières* (MSF) withdrew from the country after the murder of five of its staff the previous month. Those humanitarian organisations that stayed have had to accept constant curfews and restrictions of movement. Many non-governmental organisations (NGOs) now travel incognito having discarded their distinctive flags and badges. The humanitarian emblems that once served to protect them now identify them as 'legitimate targets.'

The constant attacks, with aid convoys ambushed, premises rocketed and mortared and vehicles booby-trapped, have led to a growing feeling of anguish and anger within the NGO community. No one doubts that a desperately poor country like Afghanistan needs humanitarian assistance, but many are asking whether the price being paid is too high. This is not simply a question of the value placed on human life. Most NGOs continue to refuse to accept armed guards or escorts, but the militarised environment in which they work is having an impact on their identity and the way in which they are perceived by others. In May this year a battle between police and insurgents in an eastern province of Afghanistan left several officers and one civilian dead. US helicopters fired rockets to defend a guard post, and the attackers were eventually driven off. Such attacks are almost daily occurrences in Afghanistan, but what made this one unusual was that it took place in a school supported by the Swedish Committee for Afghanistan, an NGO which had not been informed that a security post had been set up inside its project.

Today aid workers are frequently depicted by opponents of the present government of Afghanistan as part of a western plot to subjugate the Muslim world. Before I came to Afghanistan I was working as a UNHCR Protection Officer in Kosovo. A few days after the September 11th attacks in New York, I and several of my colleagues left for Afghanistan in anticipation of the human catastrophe that was to come. Sheltered by the UN flag, our independence and neutrality was, more or less, respected by all sides. After all, the Taliban regime had relied heavily on international humanitarian assistance to meet the basic needs of its subjects when it was in power. Recently this situation has changed, because although Afghanistan has endured a quarter of a century of conflict, it is only in the last couple of years that killing aid workers has become a deliberate method of waging war. It is ironic that staff of the International Committee of the Red Cross (ICRC), whose delegates are the only people to have any access to the Guantánamo Bay detainees, and who were the first to draw attention to the abuse of prisoners by the US military in Iraq, are now regularly targeted in these attacks.

Killing aid workers disrupts the delivery of humanitarian assistance and so increases the suffering of the civilian population. While it is one means of showing that parts of a country remain ungovernable, it is a tactic that anti-government forces usually disavow because it hits their own supporters as well.

In the past there was a clear distinction between long-term development – aid, emergency relief to help the victims of natural disasters, and humanitarian action during conflicts. The latter was given under terms of strict neutrality and largely regulated by the Geneva Conventions. Indeed one of the most widely understood points contained in the Geneva Conventions is the special position accorded to humanitarian organisations such as the ICRC.

MERCY

SEF

RVE

HOPE

Today, however, in an era where the vast majority of conflicts take place in the poorest countries in the world and where famines and other natural disasters are sometimes used by the protagonists in a conflict for factional advantage, these distinctions have become increasingly blurred. The challenge for humanitarian aid workers is how to maintain their impartiality in the increasingly politicised environments in which they operate.

During the 1990s some aid NGOs moved away from their traditional position of neutrality by calling for Western military intervention, for humanitarian purposes, in certain circumstances. MSF, for example, took out advertisements during the crisis in Rwanda proclaiming that 'one cannot stop a genocide with medicines!' Other organizations called for action to halt the killings in Bosnia. Aid workers now often also co-operate with the military in conflict and post-conflict zones through sheer practical necessity.

NGOs have also become increasingly reliant on government funding for their activities. The humanitarian crises of the 1990s led to a vast expansion of the size and number of NGOs as they often acted as semi-official distributors of relief. In many countries, including Afghanistan, NGOs have assumed responsibility for state-type functions such as the provision of public services, health and education. Long-term development assistance has continued to decline over the past 15 years, but there has been a big increase in spending on humanitarian relief. Much of this is now channeled through humanitarian NGOs.

Some governments have been keen to use the leverage of international assistance to promote other, more political, goals. Britain's Department for International Development, for example, links the delivery of such assistance to 'joined-up objectives', such as restoring peace and human rights in conflict and post-conflict zones. The United States Government has even more overtly called on NGOs to help US foreign policy goals and act as a 'force multiplier' of its military strategy.

Since the advent of the Bush administration and the attacks on September 11th, in particular, the 'humanitarian space' in which aid workers can operate has been steadily shrinking. Both Bush and Bin Laden have called on everyone to 'take sides' in a war, variously described as 'against terrorism' or 'for global *jihad*.'

For NGOs maintaining independence in these circumstances is difficult. Humanitarian organizations emphasize the importance of international humanitarian law because it provides a set of rules binding all sides in a conflict. One of these is that humanitarian relief should be distributed impartially and solely on the basis of need. Humanitarian actors have a right to offer their services without this being construed as a hostile, or politically partisan, act. Humanitarian organizations must also not act as instruments of any government or ally themselves with any side in a conflict. These principles are set out in the Geneva Conventions. They were reaffirmed by the International Court of Justice (ICJ), when it ruled that President Regan's support for the right-wing *Contras* in Nicaragua during the 1980s was illegal. Until recently most democratic governments accepted the need to act within this international legal framework.

The US invasion of Iraq presented many humanitarian organisations with a dilemma. Some already had programmes in the country, where they were helping the poor and vulnerable, and others quickly moved to establish them in the post-conflict environment. A few voiced concerns about being identified with an operation that violated international law and questioned whether the world's second biggest producer of oil was a natural candidate for humanitarian aid. The sums of money that the US and British Governments were prepared to pour into Iraq struck many as obscene, particularly when compared to the pitiful assistance given to much more desperate situations elsewhere in the world. Some NGOs felt that they were being treated as sub-contractors by the occupying forces and most withdrew from Iraq in the autumn of 2003 as the security situation worsened.

Afghanistan has posed a different set of dilemmas for the international aid community. The US response to September 11th was to step up support for the anti-Taliban militias of the Northern Alliance. Backed by US airpower these soon swept to power as the discredited Taliban regime collapsed. The US continued to support some of these local militias even after a new Government had been established in Kabul and in spite of the appalling human rights records of their leaders. This entrenched some warlords and led to the creation of a number of

regional fiefdoms around Afghanistan. It also convinced many that so long as they remained allies of the US in its 'war against terrorism' they could otherwise regard themselves as being above the law.

The failure of the international community to honour the military and financial commitments it initially made to Afghanistan also significantly weakened the new Government. Much of the country remains lawless and, even in the areas that they control, the police and courts are unable to protect basic human rights. Corruption is rife and opium production is booming again. Popular alienation from the Government is, in some ways, similar to the situation that led to the toppling the previous Mujahedin Government by the Taliban in the mid 1990s. It is no coincidence that this force has now re-emerged as a credible threat. For donors and the international community, restoring the rule of law in Afghanistan is increasingly seen as a vital part of the process of disarmament, political reform and social reintegration.

The Norwegian Refugee Council established a network of free legal aid centres in Afghanistan in 2003. Legal aid might not seem the first priority for a human-itarian assistance organisation in a situation where people's physical needs for food, shelter, security and basic healthcare have not been met. Nonetheless, its practical value in post-conflict situations is being increasingly recognised. Until the rule of law has been re-established, most attempts to tackle other social problems are likely to be little more than short-term palliatives.

Running a legal aid program in the absence of a rule of law is an interesting challenge. It proved possible in Afghanistan because of the existence of a highly developed system of customary law, which is largely enforced through village Shuras and Jirgas that have continued to function while the official courts have been in abeyance. Afghan customary law is often rightly criticized for failing to uphold internationally recognised human rights norms – particularly in its treatment of women. However, for many ordinary Afghans it offers a fairer, faster and more accessible system of justice than the official court system. In the long-run it seems likely that formal and informal justice mechanisms will probably continue to exist side-by-side.

The bigger problem has been to try to persuade the international community of the importance of international law and the need to abide by it even when it conflicts with short-term political expediency. The US in particular, which has the largest contingent of international troops in the country and is one of the largest international donors, has failed to give a positive lead in this regard.

For humanitarian organisations, one of the most immediate issues has been the way in which the US has deliberately blurred the lines between humanitarianism and military action. This violates international humanitarian law and, obviously, endangers humanitarian aid workers. It was one of the reasons cited by MSF for their withdrawal from the country.

Military-led provincial reconstruction teams, for example, have been deployed in many parts of the country and sometimes carry out humanitarian activities that used to be the preserve of NGOs. These are essentially 'hearts and minds' operations, used by the military to win local support. However, the soldiers concerned drive similar vehicles to those used by humanitarian organizations, often operate in plain clothes with their weapons concealed, and have been accused of using humanitarian assessment missions as a front for intelligence-gathering. In one well-publicized incident, US soldiers distributed leaflets telling people that their humanitarian assistance would be cut unless they supplied information about local Taliban activities. At one meeting I attended where such practices were criticized, one military officer responded that perhaps NGOs should also supply their own staff with weapons.

A bigger concern for most Afghans is the network of private prisons run by private militias and public officials to detain people without any reference to the courts. Such prisons are completely illegal, but are widely tolerated. Indeed the US military has established its own network to detain thousands of suspected Taliban and Al Qaeda members, incommunicado, for indefinite periods.

The Norwegian Refugee Council's legal counsellors have heard of people who quite literally disappear into US custody. With no rights of legal access, we can do little except inform the ICRC to find out if they have turned up in Guantánamo Bay. Anguished relatives wait for months with no word and, hearing nothing,

MERCY   MSH

WHO

FAO   UNICA

USAID

SERVE

PARSA

HOPE

CARE

AMI

ECHO

often assume the worst. When news broke of the prisoner abuse scandal in Iraq, many Afghans naturally concluded that the same was happening in Afghanistan.

This created a pervasive climate of fear and hatred. When I asked one Afghan judge why he had not made an official complaint after hearing accounts of two detainees who alleged to him that they had been mistreated in US military custody, he told me, only half-jokingly, that he did not want to end up in Guantánamo Bay himself.

The balance-sheet of the international community's involvement in Afghanistan is not all negative. The country enjoys far more freedom than it did under the Taliban. It has a new constitution and, for the first time in its history, a President has been elected under reasonably free and fair elections. Women, particularly in Kabul, enjoy incomparably more rights than before. The economy is booming, albeit largely due to drug money, and humanitarian aid has vastly improved the lives of the poorest and most vulnerable. Much of the country remains at peace and this has given impetus to the resumption of normal social and economic activity. Above all, the Afghans themselves have finally been given a chance to take control of their country's own destiny.

Bettina Goislard had formed a strong attachment to Afghanistan during her time there. She had learnt to speak Dari and had many Afghan friends. In the event of her death she had asked to be buried in the country and her body now lies in the British cemetery in Kabul. Most ordinary Afghans reciprocated this affection. When she was shot, local people intervened to try and save her life and arrest her killers. Concepts such as human rights, solidarity and compassion are not that difficult for most people to grasp. Unfortunately our current generation of political leaders seem to have forgotten their importance in creating a more peaceful and secure world based on an international rule of law.

Conor Foley was Program Manager of the Norwegian Refugee Council's legal aid project in Afghanistan from July 2003 to August 2004. He has previously worked for a number of human rights and refugee organisations including Amnesty International.

Conor Foley
October 2004

MERCY MSH

FAO UNICA

UNHCR WIN

USAID

CPHA CIC

JEN

GOAL

SERVE

ATCE

ALA

PARSA

HOPE

AMI

ECHO

TDH UNHCR ALA MRC

AIMS

CARE JEN COOPI GTZ

HOPE DCA JCCP OMA

SORA

WIN ADSI AMURT COW

GTZ USAID IFRC ACBA

AAA

NAC ATCE CIC UNIC

CPHA IAM PARSA IFES

UCL

MSH NCA UNDCP SCA

AMI UNCHS WHO BRAC

WHO

MC GOAL SAB ACTED

GMS SERVE TODAI UCL

MRCA

HEP ATLAS PHO ECHO

NDP CWS EMDH MDM

TODAI

CDAP UNOPS AIMS SORA

OCUS ISRA AAA MMCC

ISRA

OFID ADRA FAO MERCY

168

MAD
BSL
ATL
MAN
CAI
SYD
SIN
BKK
SEA
CDG
LHR
VIE
DAM
JFK
ATH
JED
JKT
DAD
BEG
HAN
SGN

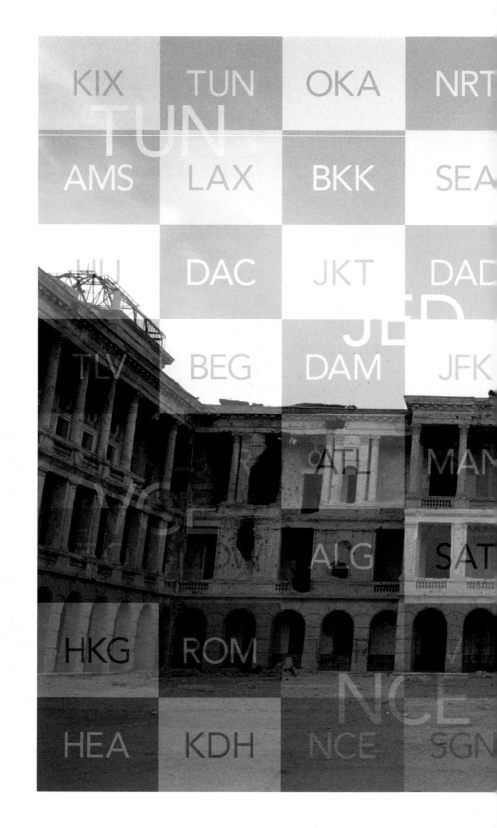

ATH KHI MLA VCE
SYD
SYD SIN WAS HAM
FRA BAH PHX BIO
ALG
LJU ZAG SOF SIN
CAS HAN
IST KBL
GVA CDG
BAH
JAA AMM PIT FUK

ACBAR	Agency Coordinating Body for Afghan Relief	
AAD	Afghan Aid	
ACF	Action Contre la Faim	
ACTED	Agence d'aide a la cooperation Technique et au Dévelopment	
AAA	Action Aid Afghanista	
ADRA	Adventist Development & Relief Agency	
ADSI	Action & Développement Solidaires International	
AED	Academy for Education Development	
AFRANE	Amité Franco Afghane	
AIMS	Information Management System (United Nations)	
ALA	Afghanistan Libre Association	
AMI	Aide Medicale International	
AMURT	Ananda Marga Universal Relief Team (Switzerland)	
ATCE	Afghan-Turk Cag Educational	
ATLAS	Action Transport Logistique Assistance Service	
BRAC	Bangladesh Rural Advancement Committee	
CARE	Coordination of Afghan Relief	
CDAP	Comprehensive Disabled Afghans Programme (United Nations)	
CHF	Community, Habitat, Finance	
CIC	Children in Crisis	
CFA	Child Fund Afghanistan	
COOPI	Cooperazion Internazional (Italy)	
CORD AID	Cord Aid (Netherlands)	
COW	Children of War	
CPHA	Chak-e-Wardak Hospital Project	
CRF	Canadian Relief Foundation	
CRS	Catholic Relief Services	
CWS	Church World Service	
DACAAR	Danish Committee for Aid to Afghanistan	
DCA	Dutch Committee for Afghanistan	
DDG	Danish De-mining Group	
DFID	Department for International Development	
DWHH/GAA	Deutsche Welthungerhilfe/German Agro Action	

EA	Euro Aid	
ECHO	European Commission Humanitarian Office	
EFCR	European Foundation for Conflict Resolution	
EMDH	Enfants du Monde Droits de l'Homme, les Droits de l'Enfant	
EMERGENCY	Life Support for Civilian War Victims	
FAO	Food and Agriculture Organisation (United Nations)	
FOCUS	Focus on the Global South	
GMS	German Medical Services	
GNI	Good Neighbours International	
GOAL	Goal International	
GTZ	Deutsche Gesellshaft fur Technische Zusammenarbeit	
HHI	Habitat for Humanity International	
HI(B)	Handicap International (Belgium)	
HI(F)	Handicap International (France)	
HEP	Help & Education Projects International Canada	
HF	Hammer Forum	
HOPE	Hope World Wide	
HNI	Health Net International	
HRW	Human Rights Watch	
IAM	International Assistance Mission	
IBC	International Blue Crescent	
ICMC	International Catholic Migration Commission	
ICRC	International Committee of the Red Cross	
IFES	International Foundation For Election Systems	
IF HOPE	International Foundation of Hope	
IFRC	International Federation of Red Cross & ed Crescent	
IHRLG	International Human Rights Law Group	
IHSF	International Health Services Foundation	
ILO	International Labour Organisation	
IMC	International Medical Corps	
INTERSOS	Intersos (Italy)	
IOM	International Organisation for Migration	
IR	Islamic Relief UK	

International Rescue Committee
Islamic Relief Agency
The World Conservation Union
Japan Centre for Conflict Prevention
Japan Emergency NGO
Kindershilfwerk Afghanistan e.V.
Kreditanstalt fur Wiederaufbau
Madera (BIA - Bureau International pour l'Afghanistan)
Mobile Mini Circus for Children
Medicins Du Monde
Mission East
Medica Mondial
Mercy Corps
Medial Refresher Courses for Afghans
Medical Relief International
Médecins Sans Frontiers
Management Sciences for Health
Norwegian Afghanistan Committee
Norwegian Church Aid
Organisation zur orderung Afghanischer Regionaler Initiativer
Ockenden International
Organisation for Mine Clearance & Afghanistan Rehabilitation
Physiotherapy & Rehabilitation Support for Afghanistan
Peace Winds Japan
Polish Humanitarian Organisation
Relief International
Solidarite Afghanistan Belgium
Save the Children
Swedish Committee for Afghanistan
Save the Children - Japan
Save the Children - Sweden
Save the Children - USA
Save the Children - UK

SDC	Swiss Agency for Development and Cooperation
SERVE	Serving Emergency Relief & Vocational Enterprises
SGAA	Sandigal Afghanistan Appeal
SFL	Shelter for Life International
SNI	Shaelet Now International
SORA	Support Organisation for Refugees of Afghanistan
SOLIDARITES	Aide Humanitaire d'Urgence
SWISS PEACE	Afghan Civil Society Forum
TEAR FUND	Tear Fund Disaster Response Team
TDH	Terre Des Hommes
TODAI	Relief Organisation in Japan
UCL	Leonard Cheshire Centre of Conflict Recovery
UMCOR	United Methodist Committee on Relief
UNAMA	United Nations Assistance Mission in Afghanistan
UNCHS	United Nations Centre for Human Settlement
UNDCP	United Nations Drug Control Programme
UNDP	United Nations Development Programme
UNESCO	United Nations Educational Scientific and Cultural Organisation
UNFPA	United Nations Famiily and Population Agency
UNHCR	United Nations High Commission for Refugees
UNICA	United Nations International Committee for Afghanistan
UNICEF	United Nations International Childrens Emergency Fund
UNMSA	United Nations Special Mission to Afghanistan
UNOCHA	United Nations Office for Coordination of Humnaitarian Relief
UNOCHA/RMAC	United Nations Regional Mine Action Centre
UNOPS	United Nations Office for Project Services
USAID	US Agency for International Development
WFP	World Food Programme (United Nations)
WHO	World Health Organisation (United Nations)
WIN	World in Need
WORLD VISION	World Vision International Christian Relief
ZOA	Zust Oust Asia
ZUFLUCHT	Revolution One (Switzerland)

Murder Trial

Murder Trial

DVD, colour, sound, 12 minutes.

On 15 October 2002 Langlands & Bell attended a murder trial at the Supreme Court in Kabul. The accused was a man called Abdullah Shah who was being tried with his accomplice Mohammed Arif in open court for murdering dozens of people. His victims included three of his own wives, who he set fire to and threw into a well, and five of his own children – some of whom he butchered, by cutting off their ears and noses.

Shah was a notorious 'commander' during the civil war who served in the Hezb-i-Islami faction with another wanted commander ▮▮▮▮▮ who 'ruled' the town of Sarobi east of Kabul. Shah gained the title '▮▮▮▮▮▮▮▮' for savaging travellers with his teeth before killing them while collecting tolls. At the end of the trial he was sentenced to death. If the decision of the court is upheld, it will be the first judicial execution in Afghanistan since the fall of the Taliban.

Langlands & Bell videoed the trial from their seat in the courtroom with a hand held camera. Shah's activities wrought destruction in the lives of numerous ordinary people. In the film the protagonists, and the procession of witnesses who mount the stand in turn to testify, seem to symbolise the struggle of the Afghan people to come to terms with the terrible devastation of the past twenty three years as they try to rebuild their lives.

Postscript
On Tuesday 27th April 2004 the BBC reported that Abdullah Shah had been executed by a single bullet to the head in the Pul-e-Charki prison, Kabul, during the previous week.

Amnesty international commented, *Abdullah Shah was denied even basic human rights... execution may have been an attempt by powerful political players to eliminate a key witness to human rights abuses.*

The office of Hamid Karzai the president of Afghanistan commented, *the president felt compelled by the need to ensure justice to the victims.*

ABDULLAH SHAH '▮▮▮▮▮▮▮▮▮▮▮'

BLESSING THE COURT BEFORE THE PROCEEDINGS

MOHHAMED ARIF ACCOMPLICE

The Judge

The Prosecutor

READING THE CHARGES

SHAH RESPONDS TO THE CHARGES

THE WITNESSES

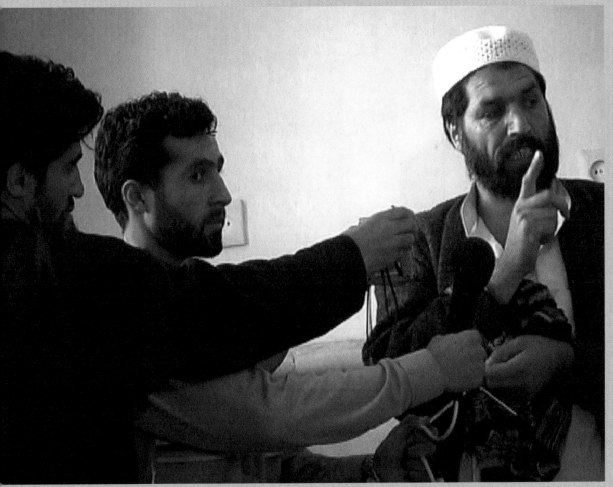

Shah responds to the witnesses' testimony

THE VERDICT OF THE COURT

Low Graphics version | Change edition

Search

About BBC News | Feedback | Help

BBC NEWS UK EDITION

WATCH/LISTEN TO BBC NEWS

News Front Page
World

Last Updated: Tuesday, 27 April, 2004, 11:57 GMT 12:57 UK

✉ E-mail this to a friend   🖨 Printable version

Afghan state executions restart

Africa
Americas
Asia-Pacific
Europe
Middle East
South Asia
UK
England
Northern Ireland
Scotland
Wales
Business
Politics
Health
Education
Science/Nature
Technology
Entertainment

Have Your Say
Magazine
In Pictures
Week at a Glance
Country Profiles
In Depth
Programmes

BBC SPORT
BBC WEATHER
CBBC news
BBC ON THIS DAY

LANGUAGES
اردو
हिन्दी
বাংলা
MORE >

Afghanistan has carried out its first execution since the fall of Taleban hardliners more than two years ago.

A former military commander convicted of murder was killed at a jail outside Kabul last week, it emerged on Tuesday.

Abdullah Shah received a single shot to the head after President Karzai gave his approval, the attorney general's office told the Associated Press.

Amnesty International, the human rights group, says Abdullah Shah was denied even basic standards of fairness.

The group said it feared the "execution may have been an attempt by powerful political players to eliminate a key witness to human rights abuses".

Abdullah Shah served under another commander, Zardad, in the 1992-96 civil war, and earned the nickname ███████ for attacks on travellers along the road between Jalalabad and Kabul in the 1990s.

'Justice'

Afghan officials say Abdullah Shah, executed at Pul-e-Charkhi jail, was convicted on 20 counts of murder in special court proceedings in October 2002.

He was found guilty of killing one of his wives by pouring boiling water over her body.

Another wife, who said he had tried to burn her to death after dousing her with petrol, was one of those who testified against him.

The court heard Abdullah Shah murdered his baby daughter by banging her repeatedly against a wall, officials say.

President Karzai had signed

> 66 **The president felt compelled by the need to ensure justice to the victims** 99
>
> Presidential spokesman Jawed Ludin

AFGHANISTAN'S FUTURE

PRESSURES ON THE GOVERNMENT

Donor boost
Should President Karzai be satisfied with pledges of aid in Berlin?

Aims of Berlin conference
Drugs threat
The security nightmare
Disarming the militias
Resurgent Taleban

PHOTO ESSAYS
Afghanistan in pictures: 1
Afghanistan in pictures: 2

BACKGROUND
War crimes unpunished
The future of democracy
Profile: Hamid Karzai
Country profile

TOP SOUTH ASIA STORIES NOW
Afghanistan resumes state executions
BJP mulls over India's exit polls
Concern over freed child soldiers
Afghan workers 'gunned down'

REUTERS 🌐

BC-AFGHAN-COMMANDER-DEATH
Afghan death sentence for "███████████" commander
By Sayed Salahuddin
KABUL, Oct 15 (Reuters) — An Afghan tribunal sentenced one of the
country's most notorious commanders to death on Tuesday for murdering
dozens of people including three of his wives and five of his children.
The court judge said Abdullah Shah could appeal against the sentence
and President Hamid Karzai's approval for the death sentence was
needed.
The court also sentenced his alleged accomplice, Mohammad Arif, to
prison for 10 years. Both of the accused, who appeared in shackles
before an open court, pleaded not guilty and rejected the charges
against them.
Afghanistan's chief justice and head of the Supreme Court, Fazl Hadi
Shinwari, has already demanded Karzai award the death penalty to Shah.
If the court's decision is upheld, it would be the first official
execution in Afghanistan since the fall of the hardline Islamic Taliban
regime late last year.
"We don't accept the decision. We will appeal against the court's
verdict," Shah told the court judge.
When Afghanistan was in the grip of civil war in the 1990s, Shah
served as a commander with another wanted warlord ██████ from the Hezb-
i-Islami faction led by Gulbuddin Hekmatyar, officials said.
According to Shinwari, Shah hails from Paghman, a village outside
Kabul city. He earned the title "███████████" for biting and killing
travellers who refused to pay duties to ███████, who ruled the town of
Sarobi east of Kabul in the 1990s.
Shah's fourth wife is among several petitioners against her 43-year-
old husband, court officials said.
"He is famous as '███████████' and we have witnesses and petitions
from a number of people against him. He himself has confessed to having
killed his family members and he should be punished severely," Shinwari
said in a recent interview.
"Islamic laws propose execution and that is what I am demanding is
done."
The Taliban attracted stern international criticism for applying harsh
Islamic punishment, including executing murderers, during its five
years in power. Many executions were carried out in public.
The Taliban also chopped off the hands of thieves, lashed people
caught taking drugs and drinking alcohol and stoned or lashed
adulterers. The punishments had the effect of reducing crime during
Taliban rule. Reut08:13 10-15-02

Due to the trial of Faryadi Sarwar Zardad currently in progress at the Old Bailey, this work has been removed temporarily following legal advice.

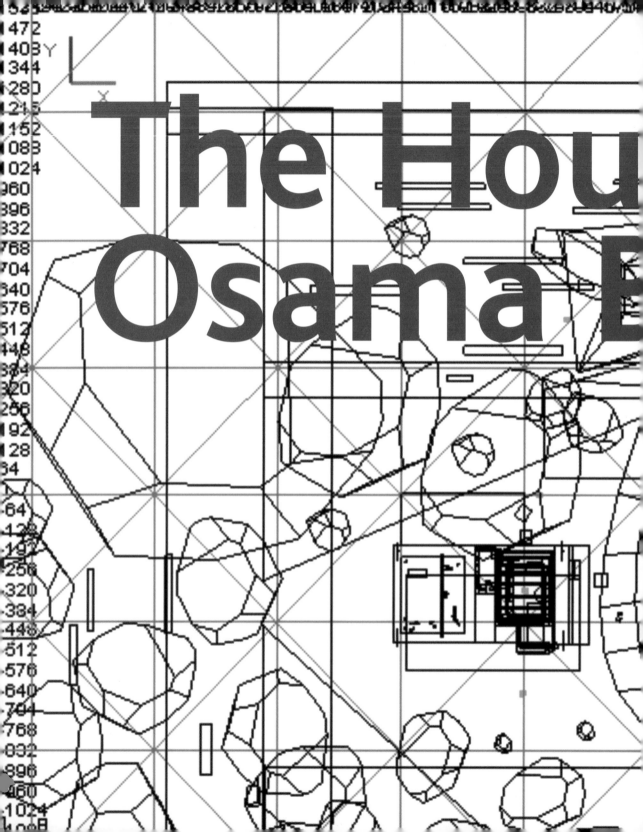

The Hou
Osama B

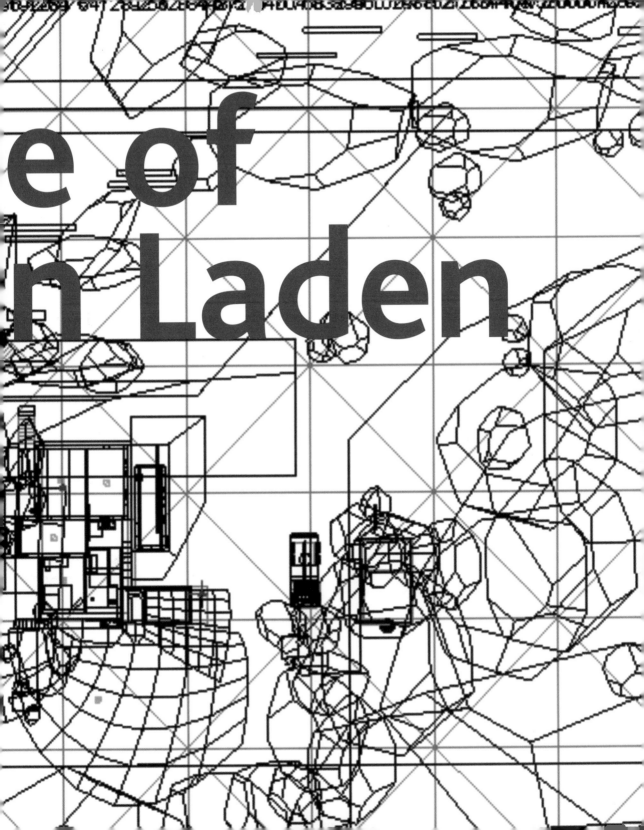

Technology

The House of Osama bin Laden is an interactive digital animation made by Langlands and Bell with the technical collaboration of Tom Barker's V/Space Lab.

The production of the work was initially commissioned by the Imperial War Museum, London for the exhibition *Langlands & Bell – The House of Osama bin Laden* at the Imperial War Museum, London 10 April – 26 May 2003.

The House of Osama bin Laden was conceived and developed by Langlands & Bell from hundreds of photographs and measurements taken by the artist's when they visited a house formerly occupied by Osama bin Laden at Daruntah in Eastern Afghanistan in October 2002.

The artists collaborated with Tom Barker's V/SpaceLAB to produce an interactive digital model of Osama bin Laden's domain. The model allows "visitors" to explore the house and it's surroundings virtually, interacting by means of a joystick.

The House of Osama Bin Laden makes pioneering use of computer games technology to create a three dimensional environment that allows visitors to walk freely around it's digital world. The underlying technology of the work is based on a computer game called *Quake*, by ID software. Hundreds of images compiled by Langlands & Bell have been digitised and placed into a customised set of special effects libraries designed by Tom Barker called V/SpaceLAB. The V/SpaceLAB libraries facilitate transparency, translucency, lighting and all the requirements to make a computer world convincing.

Images in V/SpaceLAB are treated as digital "wallpaper" textures and "wrapped" around the "3 dimensional objects" in the virtual model. The design mixes real and apparent 3D objects and surfaces. Finally the model is saved and processed, turning an ASCII text file into a computer binary file to be run by the Quake game engine. The binary file has additional information in it to describe shadow and sunlight.

The House of Osama bin Laden

Interactive Digital Animation

The House of Osama bin Laden explores ways in which evidence of the identity or presence of a person may be discovered, revealed, or projected, in a locality after their departure. In the aftermath of September 11 Osama bin Laden has attained a quasi mythical status. At the time of making this work, the question remains: is he alive or is he dead? Where are his remains, or where is he hiding? Would we even recognise him if we saw him? While bearing testimony to his absence, the vacant house at Daruntah becomes through art a metaphor, for the elusive presence bin Laden maintains by the fact of his disappearance.

The house stands on a promontory over looking a lake in the mountains east of Kabul. It commands a panoramic view of its surroundings and consists of several structures set in an area of rough ground littered with discarded spent and live munitions, abandoned military vehicles and rusting hardware. The buildings comprise a modest four roomed house built in the local vernacular style with a small terrace and an external kitchen lean-to, a small mosque, and a bomb shelter/bunker. The latter two buildings were added by Bin Laden specifically for his own use. The mosque is conventionally constructed out of local stone and concrete while the bunker is an unusual, partially excavated structure with walls made from stacked wooden ammunition boxes filled with rocks and earth as ballast. It is covered with an earth and stone roof set on branches strengthened with ex-Soviet truck chassis.

Architecture is one of the most tangible records of the way we live. Buildings tend to encapsulate our hopes and fears at many levels while also reflecting the persistent human will to plan events. This is evident whether we are considering the monumental edifices of the twin towers in New York, or this modest group of structures at Daruntah. In both contexts we can discover a language of intentions in the character and fabric of the structure.

AWM SAISS FAGTA

SDIG DFLP MRT

ANSA SJKDFI FAIRO

NIUFA LIST SPA

UDA UNSTA FARR

PSTAE KJLCA SHUA

IRIA CNBD PLLA

NSPLCA RUF KIAGU

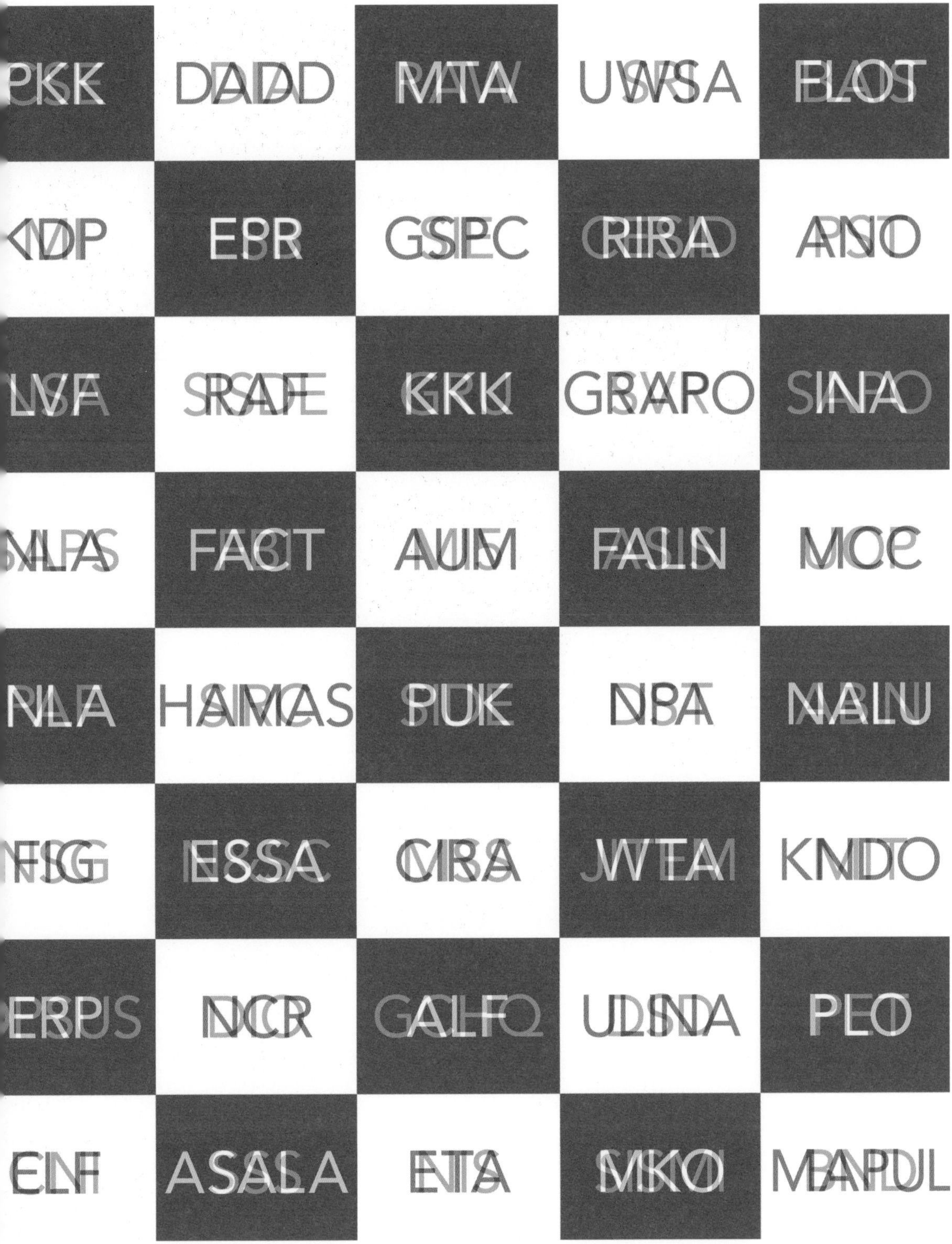

KKK

UWSA

DIE

WTA

SLA

DIS

JITEM

SIE

GID

The Aftermath of September 11 and the War in Afghanistan

The Imperial War Museum is used to people questioning the purpose of commissioning 'war artists', as if the very concept should have died out around the time of the Crimean War or at the very least at the end of the First World War. Brought up on a diet of war photography and film since the late 1930s, mesmerised by images that freeze a moment in time in perpetuity, we question whether artists still have a role to play when recording war is done so much more efficiently and with greater immediacy by journalists and cameramen equipped with the latest technology. But war art – a twentieth century phenomenon quite different from military art or history painting – is not an old-fashioned, gentler form of reportage for people who have not yet come to terms with the brutal reality of photography, video and film.

The advent of modern technology has actually removed the necessity for an artist to be a simple recorder or journalist at the same time as it has given them the tools to make creative work in new media. The technology that artists use, just like a sketchbook, is part of the process of making work, as well as an end in itself. To ask whether war artists are redundant because of the speed of modern communications is fatuous; it implies that artists are no longer equipped to respond to the modern world, and ignores the fact that artistic practice has kept pace with technological developments. But in any case, the technology thing is a red herring, because war art is not about recording news, whether on paper or canvas or with a digital camera. War art is just art, and at its best it transcends reality through the power of the imagination and shows us something we could not have envisioned for ourselves.

Some commentators want to have their cake and eat it. Artists have been criticised for being 'conspicuous by their absence' from the Iraq War, and this is seen as 'an indication that artists feel they have no place in contemporary depictions of war', as if, reluctant to be either illustrators or journalists, they can see no other creative role for themselves. In the experience of the ACC, there is no shortage of ideas, methods or approaches in the minds of artist, but they rarely involve dressing up as a soldier. Being on the front line, embedded with the armed forces, is not necessarily (indeed rarely I would say) a useful place to be if you are interrogating what you see rather than merely reflecting it.

The Art Commissions Committee, like its various predecessors in the two World Wars, sets the broad parameters for each commission but does not prescribe a theme or subject as one might for a portrait or a memorial sculpture. This comes from the artist. We assess the outline proposals that the artist makes at interview but we anticipate that their ideas may change or develop in unexpected ways as a result of their research in the field. We are looking for potential, not for certainties, for something that will surprise and challenge rather than reinforce existing stereotypes.

War is a dirty subject, perhaps especially in its aftermath, when the politics and outcomes have been laid bare. Two weeks in Afghanistan (or Kosovo or Iraq) is not a holiday: war tourists need not apply. It takes strength of mind not to be over-whelmed by the spectacle of ruins and the degradation of human life that confronts the visitor to a war zone, and retain sufficient objectivity to distil the essential elements that will add up to a meaningful response in the artist's own terms.

Langlands & Bell have said that their work 'explores systems of international communication and exchange – linked at times to issues of geo-strategic confrontation'. This a perfectly accurate description of the work they produced after their visit to Afghanistan, but it leaves out what I most admire about the way they responded to this commission. Left virtually to themselves in an extremely dangerous environment, they were tough and resourceful, and responded with open minds to every opportunity. (Can you imagine how hard it would be to get into the American airbase at Bagram if you had not met a man in the showers at the Hotel Mustafa?) They persisted in a very English way in visiting the British Embassy in Kabul and had a surreal encounter with a diplomat who clearly could not comprehend what they were doing in Afghanistan. At the same time they set their own agenda, attending the trial of Abdullah Shah, which resulted in the film ▬▬▬▬. This is both a work of art and an extraordinary historical document.

Langlands and Bell took a considerable risk in travelling to Daruntah to see Osama bin Laden's former home near the border with Pakistan. It was forbidden territory but they went just the same, making a strategic withdrawal at the very last moment. The interactive digital piece The House of Osama bin Laden is a curiously transgressive work: the war on terror meets Grand Designs. Curiosity mingles with fascination and distaste on the faces of those who dare to grasp the phallic joy stick by which one negotiates the building on screen. Its mixture of banality and threat, and the absent presence of its former owner, seem redolent of a musty but still potent fascism.

This book is a record of Langlands and Bell's experiences in Afghanistan and the work they made and are continuing to make as a result, particularly on the role of the NGOs and the military – an issue which is vividly described in Conor Foley's essay. The war on terror has rolled on to Iraq, but Afghanistan has not gone away.

Angela Weight began her career in publishing. She was a curator at Aberdeen Art Gallery in the 1970s and she has been Keeper of the Department of Art at the Imperial War Museum, and a member of the Art Commissions Committee, since 1982. She has curated many exhibitions of modern British and contemporary art at the IWM.

Angela Weight, 2004

Notes:

1
Jessica Lack, *Being There*, Frieze Contemporary Art and Culture, Issue 76, July–August 2003, pp. 62–63.

2
Op.cit

List of works

Pages 52–53
Arsenal at Daruntah: study with NGO's 2004

Pages 94–95
Black Hawks 2004 from the folio: *world wide web.af*
2004. Piezo pigment ink jet print on Hahnemuhle
Photo Rag paper 66 x 85cm; published by Alan
Cristea Gallery, London 2004

Pages 144–45
NGO: *WHO ACTED CARE* 2003. Still from dual screen
computer animation/installation and design for
flag: printed poly cotton appliqué; dimensions
variable. Collection: Imperial War Museum London

Pages 148–49
NGO: *MERCY SERVE HOPE* 2003. Still from dual
screen computer animation/installation and
design for flag: printed poly cotton appliqué;
dimensions variable. Collection: Imperial War
Museum London

Pages 152–53
Graveyard 2004 from the folio: *world wide web.af*
2004. Piezo pigment ink jet print on Hahnemuhle
Photo Rag paper 66 x 85cm; published in an edition
of 30 by Alan Cristea Gallery, London, 2004

Pages 156–57
NGO: WHO SERVE USAID CARE 2003. Still from
dual screen computer animation/installation and
design for flag: printed poly cotton appliqué;
dimensions variable. Collection: Imperial War
Museum, London

Pages 160–61
NGO: *SERVE USAID* 2003. Still from dual screen
computer animation/installation and design for
flag: printed poly cotton appliqué; dimensions
variable. Collection: Imperial War Museum, London

Pages 162–63
NGO: *AIMS WHO UCL ISRA* 2003. Still from dual
screen computer animation/installation and design
for flag: printed poly cotton appliqué; dimensions
variable. Collection: Imperial War Museum, London

Pages 164–65
Dump 2004 from the folio: *world wide web.af*
2004. Piezo pigment ink jet print on Hahnemuhle
Photo Rag paper 66 x 85cm; published in an edition
of 30 by Alan Cristea Gallery, London, 2004

Pages 166–67
The Bunker 2004 from the folio: *world wide web.af*
2004. Piezo pigment ink jet print on Hahnemuhle
Photo Rag paper 66 x 85cm; published in an edition
of 30 by Alan Cristea Gallery, London, 2004

Pages 168–69
Bunker wall 2004 from the folio: *world wide web.af*
2004. Piezo pigment ink jet print on Hahnemuhle
Photo Rag paper 66 x 85cm; published in an edition
of 30 by Alan Cristea Gallery, London, 2004

Pages 170–71
Ruined Monument 2004 from the folio: *world
wide web.af* 2004. Piezo pigment ink jet print on
Hahnemuhle Photo Rag paper 66 x 85cm; published
in an edition of 30 by Alan Cristea Gallery, London,
2004

Pages 172–73
Royal Palace 2004 from the folio: *world wide web.af* 2004. Piezo pigment ink jet print on Hahnemuhle Photo Rag paper 66 x 85cm; published in an edition of 30 by Alan Cristea Gallery, London, 2004

Pages 174–75
The Boneyard 2004 from the folio: *world wide web.af* 2004. Piezo pigment ink jet print on Hahnemuhle Photo Rag paper 66 x 85cm; published in an edition of 30 by Alan Cristea Gallery, London, 2004

Pages 176–75
Ruined Palace 2004 from the folio: *world wide web.af* 2004. Piezo pigment ink jet print on Hahnemuhle Photo Rag paper 66 x 85cm; published in an edition of 30 by Alan Cristea Gallery, London, 2004

Pages 178–79
NGO NGO's based in Kabul in October 2002. Vinyl decal on water soluble house paint. Installation view: *Landscapes After The Battle*, Centre d'Art La Panera, Lleida, Spain, 2004

Pages 180–81
NGO Flags. Installation view: *Landscapes After The Battle*, Centre d'Art La Panera, Lleida, Spain, 2004

Page 182
NGO. Dual screen computer animation/installation; *Landscapes After The Battle*, Centre d'Art La Panera, Lleida, Spain, 2004

Page 183
NGO Flag. Installation view: *Friendly Fire*. TENT Rotterdam 2004

Pages 184–85
The House of Osama bin Laden. Installation view: (left to right) *United Nations* 1990, *NGO* 2003, *Frozen Sky* 1999. Turner Prize 2004. Tate Britain, London

Pages 186–87
Members of the Catterick Garrison with *Frozen Sky*, *Some Versions of Light,* Telephone Repeater Station, Brompton on Swale, Yorkshire, UK

Pages 188–89
United Nations 2004 (detail). Acrylic paint over dye sublimation print on Poly cotton, 61 x 92cm

Page 213
BBC.co.uk, web page, 27.04.2004

Page 215
Transcript of Reuters report dated 15.10.2002

Page 217
Projection screen (DVD) informing of the temporary withdrawl of the video ▮▮▮▮▮▮ from *The House of Osama bin Laden* in the Turner Prize 2004 exhibition at Tate Britain, London

Pages 218–19
The House of Osama bin Laden. Screen shot of 'game map editor', Langlands & Bell with V/Space LAB

Pages 222–77
The House of Osama bin Laden. Screen shots from
interactive animation / computer installation;
Langlands & Bell with V/Space LAB

Page 278
The House of Osama bin Laden Installation view:
Galerie Christian Nagel,Cologne 2004

Pages 280–81
Untitled (BO LA SA) #8 2003. Piezo pigment print
on Tetenal Aquarell 230gm. paper, 400 x 535mm;
published by Langlands & Bell 2003

Pages 282–83
Untitled (BO LA SA) #6 2003. Piezo pigment print
on Tetenal Aquarell 230gm. paper, 400 x 535mm;
published by Langlands & Bell 2003

Page 287
www 2000. Laser etched optical glass. 100 x 100 x
100mm; published by the Multiple Store, London

Pages 288–89
NGO Computer render of proposal for flags at the
Imperial War Museum, London March 2003. Digital
artwork: Richard Wilding

Acknowledgements

The House of Osama Bin Laden originated from a research commission, *The Aftermath of September 11 and the War in Afghanistan*, awarded to Langlands & Bell by the Art Commissions Committee of the Imperial War Museum, London in February 2002. Langlands & Bell visited Afghanistan in October 2002. As a whole The House of Osama Bin Laden comprises a collection of art works in various different media, which have been shown in exhibition venues in Europe and the US since April 2003, and now this book, which seeks to draw together the various elements and events in context, in one place.

The House of Osama Bin Laden has been a diverse and at times logistically complex project which would not have been possible without the enthusiastic support and generous participation of many individuals and organisations. Ben Langlands & Nikki Bell would like to thank the following people for contributing and giving life to the project: Harriet Logan and Simon Norfolk for invaluable information and advice about travelling in Afghanistan before we left London. Jim Williams, UNESCO Project Specialist in Kabul, for invaluable information and advice about travelling in Afghanistan once we arrived in Kabul. Steve Komarrow, Journalist on *USA Today*, for friendship, advice, and lifts in his jeep. Akbar, Malik, Tahir and Zaki for their translation, guidance and advice in Kabul, and on journeys to Bamyan and Daruntah. Tom Barker, Niki Holmes, and Andrew Sidall at 'b' Consultants V/Space LAB for their production work on the interactive digital animation The House of Osama Bin Laden; Richard Wilding for his production work on NGO and ▮▮▮▮▮▮▮▮ and for his far reaching support and technical advice throughout the whole project. Bill Woodrow and the members of the Art Commissions Committee, for their encouragement and support for the project, and Gill Smith and Roger Tolson at the Imperial War Museum, for their care, and dedication; Brenda Mc Parland, Karen Sweeney and all at IMMA for presenting the exhibition The House of Osama Bin Laden in Dublin; Edwin Carels, curator of Friendly Fire, and Arno van Roosmalen and all at TENT Rotterdam for presenting The House of Osama Bin Laden in Friendly Fire at TENT during the International Film Festival Rotterdam 2004. Henry Urbach and Christian Nagel for presenting the works The House of Osama Bin Laden and ▮▮▮▮▮▮ ▮▮▮▮ in exhibitions at their galleries in New York and Cologne in 2003/4; Lizzie-Carey Thomas, Simeon Coreless, Stephen Deuchar, Carolyn Kerr and Anna Nesbit for their invaluable assistance and advice in presenting The House of Osama Bin Laden at Tate Britain for the Turner Prize 2004; Alan Cristea, David Cleaton-Roberts and Kathleen Dempsey at Alan Cristea Gallery, London, for their support and enthusiasm for the project throughout and in particular for their advice and support during the realisation of this book; Conor Foley for Caught in the Crossfire, his vital and penetrating essay exploring the shifting territory occupied by NGOs in Afghanistan and elsewhere; Herman Lelie and Stefania Bonelli for the dedication and enthusiasm they have brought to the task of designing this book, and finally and most wholeheartedly to Angela Weight, Keeper of the Department of Art at the Imperial War Museum, London, for inviting us to take up a commission which has proved to be one of the most challenging and stimulating projects that we have ever worked on.

We are also indebted to the following people for their generous financial support, towards the realisation of this book: Janice & David Blackburn, John & Jill Broome, Alan Cristea, Lord & Lady Egremont, Stuart Evans, Alex & Val Hackel, Katrin Henkel, Lea Simonds, and the Imperial War Museum Art Commissions Committee.

Due to the trial of the alleged Afghan warlord Faryadi Sarwar Zardad at the Old Bailey in London while this book is being prepared, certain titles and references have been altered or deleted due to legal advice.

Credits and Copyright

Caught in The Crossfire © 2004 Conor Foley

Afghan Diary Text and images © 2002/3 Langlands & Bell

██████████ Edited by Richard Wilding © 2003 Langlands & Bell

NGO Digital artwork and image sequencing by Richard Wilding © 2003 Langlands & Bell

The House of Osama bin Laden Interactive Animation © 2003 Langlands & Bell and V/Space LAB

The Aftermath of September 11 and the War in Afghanistan © 2004 Angela Weight

NGO and ██████████ Courtesy of Langlands & Bell and the Trustees of the Imperial War Museum

NGO Photos of installation at La Panera. Courtesy Centre d'Art La Panera, Lleida, Barcelona, Spain

world wide web.af © 2004 Langlands & Bell. Courtesy of Langlands & Bell and Alan Cristea Gallery, London

Members of the Catterick Garrison with Frozen Sky, Some Versions of Light; Telephone Repeater Station, Brompton on Swale, UK © 2004 Greville Worthington

© BBC on line 2004, page 213

© Reuters, page 215

Design by Herman Lelie, Stefania Bonelli, Langlands & Bell

First published in the United Kingdom in 2004 by Thames & Hudson Ltd, 181A High Holborn, London WC1V 7QX

www.thamesandhudson.com

British Library Cataloguing-in-Publication Data
A catalogue record for this book is available from the British Library

ISBN-13: 978-0-500-28565-7
ISBN-10: 0-500-28565-7

Supported by the Imperial War Museum

Printed and bound in the Netherlands by Lecturis